920 Ob14o 70-3263
The Observer, London.
Observer profiles

0 0005 0056682 6

Y0-DFQ-557

CT
120
.O2
1970

Observer (London, England)

Observer profiles.

920 Ob14o

DUE

KCK COMM. JR. COLL. LIBRARY
727 Minnesota Ave.
Kansas City, Kansas 66101

PRINTED IN U.S.A.

OBSERVER
Profiles

OBSERVER
Profiles

With an Introduction by
IVOR BROWN

Biography Index Reprint Series

BOOKS FOR LIBRARIES PRESS
FREEPORT, NEW YORK

Copyright © 1948 by The Observer

Reprinted 1970 by arrangement

STANDARD BOOK NUMBER:
8369-8022-0

LIBRARY OF CONGRESS CATALOG CARD NUMBER:
78-117330

PRINTED IN THE UNITED STATES OF AMERICA

CONTENTS

INTRODUCTION BY IVOR BROWN — 9

LEADERS OF GREAT BRITAIN
David Lloyd George — 13
Stanley Baldwin — 17
Winston S. Churchill — 20
C. R. Attlee — 25

DIPLOMACY OLD AND NEW
Ernest Bevin — 28
Molotov — 33
Andrei Gromyko — 36
Hector McNeil — 39
Count Sforza — 42

GREAT POWERS
Joseph Stalin — 46
King Ibn Saud — 50
Jawaharlal Nehru — 53
General Franco — 57

WESTMINSTER GALLERY
Sir Stafford Cripps — 60
Quintin Hogg — 64
Harold Wilson — 67
Aneurin Bevan — 70
Edith Summerskill — 73
Isaac Foot — 76
Lord Winterton — 79

CONTENTS

PERIOD PIECES
Senator Truman : 1944	82
General De Gaulle : 1943	86
Stanislaw Mikolajczyk : 1944	90
Trygve Lie : 1945	93
'Little Monty' : 1942	96

VICEROYS
Lord Wavell	99
Earl Mountbatten	102
General Robertson	106
General Clay	109

FIRST LADIES AND LEADING LADIES
Mrs Roosevelt	112
Señora Perón	116
Ninette de Valois	120
Gracie Fields	124

BACKROOM BOYS
Lord Keynes	128
Sir John Anderson	132
Sir Wilfrid Eady	135
Lord Beveridge	138
Sir John Boyd Orr	141
Dr Charles Hill	144

CONTENTS

MINDS

Bernard Shaw	147
H. G. Wells	151
Gilbert Murray	154
Arnold Toynbee	157
Benedetto Croce	160
C. G. Jung	163
Thomas Mann	166
T. S. Eliot	170

TRANSATLANTIC

Henry Wallace	174
Senator Vandenberg	178
John L. Lewis	181
Walt Disney	184

POST-WAR EUROPE

Jean-Paul Sartre	187
Kurt Schumacher	191

MOMENTS MUSICAUX

Toscanini	194
Richard Strauss	198
Hindemith	201
Benjamin Britten	205

INTRODUCTION

By IVOR BROWN

THIS SELECTION of Observer *Profiles* has been made in answer to considerable demand. The work of choosing and editing has not been easy. When world history is being made with the speed and fury of a jet plane, reputations come and go, men's achievements are suddenly and vastly increased, and news values are entirely transformed within a few days. Some of these *Profiles*, though all have been revised, of course, for book publication, will be a little out of date when they appear in book form. That is inevitable. But new facts will not, I believe, much affect the existing valuations.

These studies of the notable and notorious have never been written to a definite pattern. The methods have been as various as the authors. The general aim has been an objective portrait of any man or woman who is making or marring history, lightly informative as to biographical facts, vivid in style, but calm and just in the valuation of the subject's work and character. Brevity there had to be. More than ever now does the journalist, prisoned in his tiny wartime sheet, agree with certain metaphysicians that time and space are no figments or conditions of our thinking but realities indeed. Often these *Profiles* had to be written quickly: always concisely. Naturally, in that case, the writer could touch only certain facets of a great and versatile career. His work was one of selection and self-denial. Urgency never handicaps a well-trained and efficient journalist: the necessity of jumping to it has produced the finest of despatches, and 'leaders' are often the better for having to 'cease upon the midnight' and go warm to print before the qualifying mind and prudent afterthought start to insert the dull 'perhaps', the hesitant 'it well may be', the chilly and cautious paraphrases of the hand afraid to strike.

INTRODUCTION

Up to a point compulsion to be brief does writers no harm and in some cases it does much good. But where a man has a big, familiar, and favourite subject, knows it to the core, and has the essence of it in heart as well as brain, the limitation to less than a thousand words is galling. He has to mutilate his work in his own mind and possibly see it further cut by another hand on paper. I think most readers of this book will agree that the authors of the *Profiles* have accepted the hard conditions of the job and practised the art of condensation with fidelity and skill.

Some pieces will be found more pictorial than others for the very good reason that some of the subjects seemed to demand a dashing or impressionistic portrait, while others invited the realism of a sober chronicle. Double danger faces the *Profile* writer: he may fall to the temptation of easy scoring and brightness at any cost. Or he may, because he does indeed greatly honour and revere his subject, drift off into what the reader, in his remoteness, may regard and describe as a 'write-up'. I know no more odious term than 'write-up'. (When you have really tried to estimate with complete objectivity a man's performance on the platform, field, stage, or paper, to receive a letter saying 'thank you for the write-up' is to cause much grinding of the teeth in any sensitive journalist.) The judgment in these *Profiles* may be deemed to err on the side of gentleness. But I trust that nobody will call them 'write-ups'. They are meant to be brief chronicles, with interpretation and assessment added.

They have been very popular, a fact I can the more frankly stress because they were no creation of mine, having been introduced before my editorship of *The Observer* began. I gladly continued them. Biography is nearly always 'a good seller', for more people are interested in people than are interested in theories and principles. But there are other reasons than easy popularity for publishing these studies of character and career. Carlyle said 'history is the essence of innumerable biographies', and that point of view would be strongly countered by those who believe in the economic interpretation of events. For them

INTRODUCTION

history is the essence of innumerable pressures, pressures of hunger and misery, of tenacity and greed. There will always be two schools of history. One chronicler will have his eye on the Man, the other on the Mass. One will respond to the power of the individual, for good or ill, to set movements and myriads stirring: the other will see that individual as the inevitable product of the economic, racial, and religious stresses of the time. Two people, for example, might argue interminably as to whether Hitler made Nazism or whether Nazism is inherent in German character and, being aggravated by the Peace of Versailles and the great depression of the early 'thirties, had, of necessity, to make its Hitler.

I have no intention of intervening in this age-long dispute. All I can say is that, whatever power you attribute to the social force as against the individual leader, the latter must be an engrossing subject to any student of the splendours, ardours, and endurances as well as of the crimes, follies, and misfortunes of mankind. If the Hour, or the Movement, throws up the Man, the Man certainly affects the following minutes and gives a twist to the motions of the Movement of tomorrow. So we can accept Carlyle's judgment at least as far as the newspaper is concerned. Trends, forces, principles it tries, in its leading and special articles, to analyse and to shape. But its news columns are, as E. C. Bentley said of biography, 'about chaps', or the doings and destinies of 'chaps'. The *Profile*, relating 'chaps' to their childhood, training, racial and cultural inheritance, and social influences of all kinds, does to some extent bridge the gap between history as a Portrait Gallery and history as a Science of Social Dynamics.

With that I leave this collection to the reader, only observing that I alone am guilty of keeping him waiting—and that, I hope, not long. The Profilers, regular journalists, occasional journalists, and members of other professions, have been swift by compulsion and as rapid in drawing conclusions as in making approach to their themes. To them I would like to express the gratitude of *The Observer* for their constant readiness to supply anonymous as well as speedy and exacting service.

LEADERS OF GREAT BRITAIN

DAVID LLOYD GEORGE

SCIENCE performs miracles daily but it can neither provide nor explain the force of nature called David Lloyd George. Nothing in his ancestry would have foretold his career. A century hence historians will variously expound it. He enjoyed none of the advantages of Eton or Harrow, but a shoemaking uncle, in whose house he was entered, proved to be a first-class private tutor. He went neither to Oxford nor to Cambridge but to a Welsh Baptist chapel and a village debating society and was immersed in the Bible, Nonconformity, and the Gladstonian tradition. As a young lawyer he showed from the first a defiant audacity in the courts, criticised his 'betters' in the press, became a county council alderman at twenty-six, and a radical Member of Parliament at twenty-seven. He had to earn his own living and was entirely without influence other than his abilities could command. He not only did not belong to the governing class: he was so much an outsider that Mayfair was certain he had no manners, so thick was the slime with which he plastered his 'Limehousing' speeches. He opposed the Boer War and countenanced Passive Resistance to the Balfour Education Act of 1902.

He was never in a minor parliamentary office but went straight to be President of the Board of Trade under Campbell-Bannerman in 1906, and two years later was Chancellor of the Exchequer and talking of robbing hen-roosts. In both offices he surprised the critics by displaying qualities of action which do not normally go with those of a brilliant rhetorician. It may be true, as Asquith said, that Lloyd George and Mr Churchill 'can only think talking', but Mr Churchill's verdict on Lloyd George is no less true: 'He was the greatest master of the art of getting things done and of putting things through that I ever knew; in fact no British politician in my day has possessed half his competence as a mover of men and affairs'.

At the Treasury he saw that finance could be used as a constructive instrument of reform and he launched the Liberal Party on a social programme which, had it not been interrupted by the war, would most certainly have anticipated most features of the Beveridge Report. Because of an abnormal gift of improvisation he has been charged with having no basic philosophy, and there is a sense in which this is true, as his readiness to use all parties shows; but he had always been a radical democrat in principle and a New Dealer in practice, more akin to Franklin Roosevelt than to Woodrow Wilson: at once an opportunist and an optimist, a supple and nimble negotiator, unhampered by precedents, swift to exploit the mistakes of opponents, ready to embark on large schemes without a paralysing attention to their details, which he left where they belong —to the Civil Servants.

His reluctance to enter the war in August, 1914, was resolved by the German threat to Belgium and once war was declared he wrought with untiring energy first at the Treasury and then at the Ministry of Munitions and the War Office. No subordinate office could contain or content him. His pace was faster, his sensibilities were more acute, his transmitting and receiving antennae more numerous, than those of his colleagues. Holstein's comparison of Bismarck to a conjuror with five balls in the air at once, fitted Lloyd George. He was a whole coalition of diverse qualities in himself, intensely and simultaneously interested in all fronts, home and foreign, naval and military, sacred and secular. Of no Prime Minister has it been truer that nothing human was alien to him.

Early in his electioneering career at Caernarvon a Conservative critic had complained sarcastically that the ideas of the youthful candidate were 'as boundless as the Empire itself'. Now they spanned the world, and the barriers of party could not confine his compelling energy. He, more than anyone else, was responsible for the Coalition Government of May, 1915, and his impatience with Asquith's direction of the war ultimately brought him to the Premiership in December, 1916. Just as few rich men like to look back on the ways in which they made their first hundred thousand, so few occupants of high political office are proud of every step on their way to the summit. Certain it is that Lloyd George was always a bigger and a better statesman when loaded with the tremendous responsibilities of office than when burdened with leisure outside.

Within a few weeks of his elevation he did more to change the machine of government than any Prime Minister since Walpole by his creation of the War Cabinet, the two Secretariats, the new Ministries. He infused his own energy into all parts of the war machine; he learnt from colleagues; he listened to mutinous juniors in the Services and conquered the submarine. He had an actor's emotional force and an artist's concentration. The flattery of 'society' could not corrupt him. He was too humorous to be vain about himself, and no Prime Minister laughed more deliriously at a good joke or a comical situation; his outbursts of passion, like Napoleon's, were rarely allowed to rise above his chin. During the 'stunned pessimism' of the U-boat danger, when hope died down in others, it shone in him like a pillar of fire. Of course he made mistakes, some hard to forgive, and chiefly after the war: the 1918 election, the deference in Paris to the Northcliffe telegrams, the encouragement of the Greeks before Chanak.

How hard it was to prove him wrong he demonstrated through seven volumes of his *War Memoirs*. They are not the work of an impartial Temperley and Gooch but the case for the defendant by the solicitor who has possession of all the documents. The only drawback to the incomparable vigour of their thirty-five hundred pages is the author's 'monotonous infallibility'. What Cleon said of the Athenians is true of Lloyd George: he was too clever by half.

On 23 October 1922 he paid his last official visit as Prime Minister to the King and at four o'clock that afternoon 'the man who won the war', as Hitler once described him, walked out of 10 Downing Street alone, with his coat collar turned up, swinging a single golf club, a parting gift from a janitor, happy as a sand boy. Nobody in England that day imagined that the Prime Minister who for years had filled the world with his name and fame would never come back. His life had been full of surprises and this was the greatest. In that same week the Fascists marched on Rome and the King of Italy made way for Mussolini.

At home old party rancours revived. The Liberal Party dissolved into fragments; the Labour Party lost its first fine careless rapture; the Conservatives relapsed into Safety First. The mood of the country had changed. The hour for national tranquillity had struck and, with occasional alarms like the General Strike, it lasted nearly twenty years, almost long enough to prove that it was a synonym for treason. Lloyd George was far from being a retired or even a reticent volcano; from time to time he burst forth with incendiary pamphlets and speeches on planning, the land, the coal industry, unemployment. Today these heretical fireworks look like becoming the orthodox street lamps of the New Britain. But in the 'thirties there were still many old scores against him. He had often lashed his opponents with merciless, if picturesque, invective, and he got back what he gave.

The fires of these ancient controversies are silent in dust and ashes. We think of him as he stood on the bridge, the pilot who weathered the storm, as Canning said of Pitt. No one who watched him then, day by day, disciplined, dauntless, and determined on victory, will let 'gratitude sleep' or lightly suffer any criticism of him from any quarter whatsoever.

STANLEY BALDWIN

THE last war, like that of 1914, is historically a Great Divide. Those who retired from the centre of the political stage before the guns began are now viewed in retrospect as shapers of a world which is no more ours than that of Melbourne or Russell.

Earl Baldwin of Bewdley relinquished the Premiership in the spring of 1937. In his time he grasped nettles that have a sting in them still: mines, tariffs, India, for instance. But we were never truly at bay. The great terrors were not at hand. Stanley Baldwin's premierships, although enlivened by three first-class emergencies (General Strike, Economic Crisis, Abdication), were relatively a phase of sunset tranquillity. His personality always had a fine amber glow. None other could have rounded off his period so unobtrusively.

Baldwin has often been depicted as a simple, uncomplicated soul. Nothing could be farther from the truth. The man's nature and career are made up of strata which complement and sometimes contradict one another.

It was his delight, as we know, to get away whenever he could from the fevers and petrol fumes of Westminster; to put on the tweeds of the gentleman farmer and go pottering in Worcestershire orchards and pig-yards. We were invited by the propagandists to picture the P.M. as a man with his elbows on a five-barred gate, pipe in mouth, ready at any moment to orate movingly about wild anemones in April woods, the smell of autumn wood-smoke and other beauties of This England. Such was the increasingly popular image. At the finish it cancelled out Stanley Baldwin's industrial origins and City affiliations. We forgot the ancestral ironworks, the mines, the docks, the bank, and the railways which, until he first took junior ministerial office at the age of fifty-one, formed the main fabric of his life.

Founded by Stanley Baldwin's great-grandfather and furthered by successive sons, the foundries and forges at Wilden, near Bewdley, were run with a paternalism which survived limited company status. At Wilden, it seems, humanity came

OBSERVER PROFILES

first. Old gentlemen who had outlived their industrial usefulness were allowed to sit on wheelbarrow handles smoking their pipes all day. In the early 1920s, with industrial trouble on the boil elsewhere, Baldwins' workmen presented their principal with a china loving-cup for wartime generosities.

It was Stanley Baldwin's hope as Prime Minister that the Wilden spirit might some day be a tempering factor throughout the land. His Commons plea in 1925 for a new industrial amity and spiritual co-partnership—'Give us peace in our own time, O Lord!'—made many search their hearts. Little more than a year later the spiritual co-partners were at each others' throats. The General Strike was on. In the thick of it Mr Baldwin said, 'Everything I care for is being smashed to bits at this moment. . . . I shall pick up the bits. I shall begin again'. Even to certain of the Premier's sympathisers, the repressive Trades Dispute Bill of 1927, as originally drafted, seemed an odd sort of olive branch, a questionable way of picking up bits. Was peace in our time jettisoned? The General Strike, explained Mr Baldwin sadly, had changed the situation.

The record is rich in antitheses. Baldwin once said his mind moved slowly. In that case the tortoise had been curiously addicted to leaps in the dark. His impetuous appeal to the country on Protection at the end of 1923 'let in Labour', as the saying went, Ramsay MacDonald's Administration being the net result. He impulsively underwrote Dominion Status as India's ultimate goal before his Party as a whole had quite risen to the idea; and hastily approved—before dropping it like a hot potato—the Hoare-Laval proposal for the partition of Abyssinia. His partiality for old times and old ways was unabashed. He looked wistfully back to the days when businessmen in Worcestershire corresponded by canal barge with their fellows in Bristol and it took ambassadors' despatches three weeks to reach Whitehall. In those days, as he properly pointed out, statesmen had time and to spare for the weighing of great issues. Yet it was this foe of the newfangled who sponsored the 'Flapper Vote', a reform which helped to defeat his Party at the polls in 1929.

STANLEY BALDWIN

No Premier has been more modest about his talents. On arriving at No. 10 from the Palace in 1923 as Bonar Law's successor, he told reporters who offered congratulations that they'd do better to pray for him instead. Yet, when it came to leading a revolt (e.g. against the Lloyd George Coalition at the Carlton Club in 1922) or crushing one (e.g. Col. Gretton's ill-fated move against his leadership at the Caxton Hall in 1930), nobody could be more serenely convinced of his high mission or his fitness for it. In the same paradoxical way, when it came to sitting on facts whose disclosure he deemed inexpedient, the blunt and forthright 'Stan' of the election posters could be 'cagey' with the best. At the election of 1935 he refrained from putting the full rearmament programme before the electors. The temper of the country, he explained later, was too 'pacific' to warrant any such candour.

But political divagations are no key to what has sometimes been called the enigma of Stanley Baldwin. His knowledge of English literature was wide and deep: he was nourished and comforted by Johnson, Jane Austen, Scott, Wordsworth, and Hardy. He awoke the public to the rare talent of Mary Webb. Essentially native, he was shy of foreigners and was a warm friend of the Anglicans. He was quixotically generous. In 1919 he gave as a thank-offering for victory one-fifth of his private fortune to the Government. The paternal touch was further exercised, though in quite a different way, when Edward VIII renounced the Throne in 1936. A delicate and dangerous situation was handled with complete mastery. In the manner of a particularly nice father who knows how to be stern when he must, Mr Baldwin spoke to the right people in the right way at the right moments. And a constitutional nightmare disappeared overnight.

It is doubtful whether any Prime Minister ever enjoyed greater good will in his day. In his stocky person Stanley Baldwin summed up the moods and interests of millions. When a leader does that his tactical infelicities are freely pardoned and in his closing years his countrymen, forgetting old feuds, wished him peace at eventide among his books at Astley.

WINSTON S. CHURCHILL

OF the forty Prime Ministers who have guided the fortunes of this country in the last two centuries the men of genius among them can be counted on our fingers. By universal acclamation of his contemporaries Winston Churchill is one of them. He is not the genius who is a narrow and concentrated specialist. He is not one man but a multitude: National and Allied leader, party leader, great speaker, great writer, painter, and bricklayer, and in all these rôles he is of imagination all compact. In all of them, also, from the day, half a century ago, when he joined the Spanish Forces in Cuba, his main preoccupation has been with war as student, soldier, and statesman. The ambition of the younger Pitt was to be a Peace Minister, but fate willed otherwise; if the inmost ambition of Churchill was to be a War Minister it has been abundantly satisfied—and justified.

On 3 August 1914, when peace and war trembled in the balance, John Morley wrote: 'Yet if there is a war, Winston will beat Lloyd George hollow, in spite of ingenious computation'. Morley's partiality for his friend misled him. Churchill's hour had not struck twelve. He who declared Labour to be not fit to govern and has since successfully harnessed to his chariot three such champing steeds as Bevin, Cripps, and Morrison, was himself in December, 1916, unfit for 'the foremost station in the greatest storm'.

Conversations about Mr Churchill soon arrive at the eighteenth century, which would not happen were the company discussing any of his immediate predecessors. In the convivial habits of that century are found his bond of union with Mr Stalin. Mr Churchill has the robust tastes of the period, a love of the garish night, of good talk, Letters, pictures. He is in his sphere as representative of the qualities Englishmen admire as Dr Johnson in his. He has depths of emotion easily brought to the surface, and amid moving demonstrations or parades tears are not far off.

He has some of the healthy vulgarity which made Marie Lloyd adored. We can hardly see Chatham making the V sign to all and sundry. He is as competent as Pitt and as generous as Fox, with more staying power than either. Pitt died before he was fifty and Fox before he was sixty. Churchill commands the rhetoric of these earlier Parliamentarians, but is less spontaneous, more studied and polished. The audience has changed. The House of Commons today prefers an expository conversational manner. *Into Battle* opens with a good example—the speech condemning the surrender of the Irish Treaty ports, May, 1938.

Mr Churchill is not a slave to political theories or abstract philosophies. In assuming the leadership of the Tory Party he summed up the causes he had always served: the maintenance of the enduring greatness of Britain and her Empire and the historical continuity of our island life. In earlier days he sat at the feet, or at any rate the aesthetic luncheon table, of the Webbs and imbibed the fruitful conception of the National Minimum. He has deserted parties, but that is not the same as disloyalty to the truth. He has sometimes been wrong—an irresistible gift, Anatole France called it. 'The world decides only in favour of those who are sometimes wrong.' The Abdication, for example. He has the eighteenth-century gentleman's dislike of money and rarely refers to his period as Chancellor of the Exchequer. He may know a little more than his father about the little dots, but in 1925, with others, he went wrong on the Gold Standard. Unlike Pitt, he has not borrowed dear in wartime.

No one is more conscious than Mr Churchill of the mysterious unfurling of the scroll of human destiny, and he has told us that a man's contribution to his life story is continually dominated by an external superior power. He has also confessed that the hardest struggle of all is with oneself. Fierce and brilliant as his political apprenticeship had been, he was at forty-two still an improver, with much to learn in self-control. Nature endowed him with a profusion of gifts: the charm of entire naturalness, an iron capacity for work, a mastery of detail, rare powers of speech by tongue and pen, an all-consuming ambition. Vision and courage he had in plenty.

These gifts he exercised and matured as Head in turn of eight of the great Departments of State.

He was no sooner in charge of an office than the remotest typist was aware of his arrival, and presently masterly State papers began to reach the Cabinet Office, remarkable for their sinewy prose, the cumulative order and force of their argument, and the clarity and precision of their conclusions. This successful and variegated career was interrupted when Churchill was deposed from the bridge at the Admiralty to the Duchy of Lancaster, where he chafed and fumed: 'I knew everything and could do nothing'. Elected as a Conservative in 1900 he sat as a Liberal from 1906 to 1922; he left Asquith for Lloyd George in 1916, joined Baldwin in 1924, and in 1929 was turned out into the wilderness for ten years.

What were the reasons assigned for this strange and protracted expulsion of a Minister of consummate executive and parliamentary gifts? Asquith summed them up as extreme bellicosity. Could he add prudence to audacity, asked Lloyd George. To Churchill life is not a weary pilgrimage, but a campaign, a series of campaigns. Parliamentary elections are battlefields; labour strikes are battlefields. His imagination wielded a despotic power over his mind and magnified molehills into monsters. He saw battles where none were. Sidney Street was a battlefield. On the Ulster Border in 1922 the bloodless battle of Belleek took on the semblance of Blenheim. When during the General Strike he was in charge of the *British Gazette*, messages reached the Private Secretaries begging them to detain the editor in Whitehall on any pretext, as his devastating attack on commas and full-stops drove the compositors crazy. I lift from an old diary (1926) a paragraph which illustrates his conversational fascination.

W. is a most brilliant and incessant talker—his sentences are full of colour and alliteration and military metaphors. He is always deploying guns or barrages on the coal owners or the men. He gave us last night a wonderful description of his visit to East Africa when Under-Secretary for the Colonies: the train passing through zoological gardens with rhinos and crocodiles, twenty sorts of antelopes, lions which never brushed their teeth or cleaned their claws, so that it was desirable to avoid them, lakes as big as Scotland, the mountains of the moon. Why go shooting grouse on Yorkshire moors when you can go pig-sticking in Kenya? He stuck a pig, chasing him on horseback; the spear broke in two, it was his last, so he had to shoot with a revolver. He went on to talk of Botha and Smuts, Arthur Griffith and Michael Collins, Foch and Haig, and the war. He knows all the places and dates and details, and pictures all most vividly to his listeners.

Ten years in the wilderness! Into this green Valley of Humiliation entered the Muse of Painting, and Churchill, inflamed to action in every fibre of his being, transferred his Marlburian audacity from Cabinets to canvases. To him only would it occur that painting a picture is like fighting a battle. He devotes a page to prove the resemblance. Whatever the truth of this it is certain that the course of time, the years of painting and communion with the harmonies of nature, cooled the fiery passions and supplied a prudence and patience, a judgment and proportion, hitherto not conspicuous in his composition. So when the summons came, first to the Admiralty and then to the Premiership, it was an elder statesman, mellow and refreshed, who exchanged the studio for the bridge and then took over the supreme direction of the war.

Here at last was a world war with powers of evil to stagger even his imagination and to strain his powers and energies to the uttermost. When England had need of him he was there, subduing oratory to policy, fleeting emotion to terrific and sustained purpose. No reckless phrase, no random word fell from his vigilant lips as one broadcast followed another in the year of the Battle of Britain. The severe discipline of framing innumerable speeches, memoranda and books; the animosities, controversies, impetuosities of forty years, now shrank into a few words of one syllable when France fell and England took the decision to stand alone.

In that day of disaster and grief the student, soldier and statesman stood forth as the transfigured and embattled soul, will, and voice of his country, felt and heard throughout the world. The wilderness had done its work. The Providence that watches over us had unfurled another glorious day and deed in the scroll of our destiny. Winston Churchill's greatest hour and his country's finest hour were one and indivisible.

C. R. ATTLEE

AT Cabinet meetings the Deputy Prime Minister always sits on the edge of his chair. The trick is typical of the man. It is the sign of a diffidence, a lack of confidence, perhaps better, a modesty, that must be almost unique in high politics.

Yet this is the man who, on merit, is wartime Number Two to Mr Churchill of all people. The debt owed to loyal Clem Attlee by the Prime Minister, the country, and the Labour Party, is big. The post of Deputy Prime Minister was literally made for him and he for it; he fills it without envy.

Outside the Councils of State, too, Mr Attlee is true to type. He is almost anonymous. Slight in figure, he does not stand out in a crowd. Thin in voice, he is at a disadvantage in this Broadcasting Age. He is the forgotten Minister who four years ago brought in the forgotten Bill to put all persons and all property at the nation's disposal. Who remembers that it was he in 1941 who announced the Atlantic Charter?

How is it that he can be called the 'brace' of the Coalition? Back in the Cabinet room, or at Party meetings, the answer is plainer. Puffing at his pipe, he puts sound points well and simply. He is no colourful figure or champion of stirring causes; he is the Impeccable Chairman—at a time when both Cabinet and Party, ill-sorted and on edge, much need a chairman.

Clem Attlee is the honest broker, the good man who came to the aid of his party. He was born in 1883, a comfortable middle-class boy. He was educated at Haileybury and University College, Oxford—a young Tory without much thought.

Then he went Left by going East, to Haileybury House in the East End of London to see and know the poor. He worked at the Law, but his real practice was in Socialism with the Fabians.

The way he went was the routine road from Morris and Ruskin to the Webbs, with the boys' club in Limehouse and the political meetings to put teeth and life into his doctrine. He stumped the country explaining the great Minority Report of the Poor Law Commission and National Health Insurance. He lectured in Oxford and at the new School of Economics. He knew his stuff, a practical sociologist, an assiduous Socialist, a painstaking politician, more teacher perhaps than preacher. *Honoris Causa* he was, and is, an East Ender.

The man was father to the Minister. But between, in a characteristically dutiful interlude, came the subaltern, Captain, and Major. He served in the infantry and the Tank Corps. He fought in Gallipoli, Mesopotamia, and France. In 1919 he quickly reaped what he had sown before the war. Sixteen London boroughs went Labour, and inevitably Clem Attlee, from Stepney, took the chair—Chairman of the London Labour Mayors Association. It was only a matter of time now before he took a higher chair. In 1922 he was M.P. for Limehouse. In 1923 he was Under-Secretary of State for War. He was still, as he has always stayed, little known or canvassed in the wide world of politics. Even as an East Ender he lacked to outsiders the *réclame* of Lansbury or Hackney's Morrison. He merged into a background of routine. But in 1927, when he went with the Simon Commission to India, he was much missed.

Back home again, he became Chancellor of the Duchy of Lancaster in 1929. His patient, shrewd aid to consultation was a feature at the Imperial Conference, on the Economic Advisory Council, and in the devising of an agricultural policy. The Chairman was slowly coming into his own. Finally, two years later, he was for a few months Postmaster-General.

In the crisis of 1931 Clem Attlee had no doubts. He stayed out with Arthur Henderson, J. R. Clynes, George Lansbury, and William Graham. He preferred the wilderness and his friends to the high places with Ramsay MacDonald and Jimmy Thomas. In the General Election his friends were decimated. Only Lansbury of the Labour Cabinet came back, and Clem Attlee became Deputy Leader of the Parliamentary Party. Back he went to his dogged, dutiful speech-making, in the House and up and down the country, to keep the Party in being.

In 1935 the tide began to flow again. Many ex-Ministers came back to Westminster. When Lansbury resigned the Deputy-Leader became Acting-Leader. When the Party was offered a choice for Leader between Herbert Morrison and Arthur Greenwood, they stuck to Clem Attlee, the *Tertium*

C. R. ATTLEE

Quid, the Chairman, the known quantity, the man of character. They trusted him, both politically and personally—people always do. They were not afraid of his ambitions.

The fact is that the Labour Party distrusts Leadership. The case of Ramsay MacDonald frightened it. Nor does anyone, inside or outside the Party, know where it wishes to be led. All that is certain is that the motley group has somehow to be held together. Clem Attlee is neither bigot, doctrinaire, Labour boss, nor careerist. He puts the whole before the parts. He is a Party man, not a partisan. So he keeps the caravan in line. Can he go on doing so now the crack of the Whip by Ernest Bevin is resented?

In Downing Street there is indeed a Leader. Mr Churchill needs a Chairman for the humdrum, essential work of government. The Deputy Prime Minister is also Lord President of the Council, chairman of the Ministerial Committee that sits on home affairs. He is, in these offices, the first-class captain of a first-class cricket side who is not himself a headliner. He makes men work together. He is a political catalyst.

The historians will give Clem Attlee his due, even under the shadow of Churchill, for he, too, in his own way is equally an English worthy, though not a Great One. But they will also show how his worth to us in our tangled counsels of these days is a reflection of today's discontents and frustrations. Beneath the surface of politics there is a deep surge towards progressive ways. But there is no channel to take it. The head men are too busy shoring up the banks of the old ones. While Churchill wages war, his Chairman keeps the peace behind the lines. The one, co-ordinator much more than creator, is at least as much a man of the times as the other, the captain-general.

Indeed, the committee men and the collective bargainers, Sir John Anderson, Clem Attlee, and Ernest Bevin, typify our state more even than the fighting Winston Churchill—roadmenders, not road-builders, conservatives in the true sense of the word. The fire has not gone from the people; it has from the politicians. Clem Attlee is a Fabian; it is an infinite progress to the Brave New World he believes in. But his faith is at least real; he is a man of character.

This Profile appeared during the war when Mr Attlee was Deputy Prime Minister in the Coalition Government

DIPLOMACY OLD AND NEW

ERNEST BEVIN

WHEN the new Ministers whom Mr Churchill introduced into his wartime Coalition kissed hands, the King, as is customary, asked each of them a friendly question. Mr Ernest Bevin, as the new Minister of Labour, was asked how he had gained his great knowledge of public affairs. He is said to have replied: 'It was gathered from the hedgerows of experience'.

This would come naturally from the mouth of one of Shakespeare's yeomen. From a modern politician it sounds astonishing, both as fact and as phrase. Yet it rings true of this child of nature, Mr Bevin—so rugged, simple, and monumental if looked at from afar, so gnarled, complicated, and even mysterious on closer viewing. To the world at large, Bevin is what Churchill once called him, 'a working-class John Bull'. To those close to him, he is a much stranger figure.

Perhaps the clue to understanding Ernest Bevin lies precisely in those 'hedgerows of experience'. The so-called Public Schools have shaped the characters of many more than those who attended them. Their tradition has largely created our modern type of Englishman, with his gentleness and self-control, his mild manners and habit of understatement, his well-disciplined mind and body, his modesty, decency, and restraint.

Ernest Bevin escaped all Public School influences, and he presents an exactly opposite picture: sprawling in body and untidy in mind, dictatorial in manner and exuberant in utterance, with a streak of ferocity and a fund of native shrewdness, with every human instinct alive and unblunted, rollicking in his jollity and surly in ill-humour, as cunning as a peasant and yet, withal, as genuine as nature itself. At this turning-point in British history, we have a Foreign Secretary who is unlike any of his predecessors for at least three centuries.

Ernest Bevin's father was an ordinary agricultural labourer, who died before his son was born; his mother was a village woman, who died when he was only seven. The boy went to relatives and had started to earn his keep at eleven; he became entirely self-supporting at thirteen, when he ran away from the farm and sought freedom in the nearest city, Bristol. There he became a dishwasher at a shilling a day. He was fifteen when he settled down to a steady job, driving a horse and van for a maker of mineral waters at fifteen shillings a week, with a small commission on sales. He was later to speak of the times 'when I found myself walking the streets unemployed and having to steal for my living'.

Bevin is, of course, not the only man to rise from real poverty to great eminence. What distinguishes his career from others of this kind is its steadiness and the absence of luck. It is a slow, sure progression, step by step, merit coming before recognition, recognition before power, power before fame.

Even now, his personal life has changed very little. He has always eaten well, like a labourer, but he still neither has nor wants wealth and property. He always liked to enjoy himself, and to see others enjoy themselves. Lately, when in Paris dealing with weighty affairs of state, he accidentally encountered an Englishwoman who, because of the 'travel ban', should not have been there. 'What are you doing here, dearie?' he asked, glad to hear another English voice. She answered that she was there 'for the races'. 'I wish I was', he murmured.

Not only has his career been steady; it has always remained within his class. He never aspired to be a 'bourgeois'; he helped the working class to rise, and he rose with it. This is not only a likeable characteristic; it marks him as a natural politician and leader. Never, since he became an adult, has he sought to solve his personal problem other than by social action, which would benefit his like.

He was hardly twenty when he became the honorary secretary of a 'Right to Work' Committee of Bristol's unemployed. At thirty he was the (still honorary and unpaid) chairman of the carmen's branch of the Docker's Union. Yet another ten years went by before he became nationally known as the

'Dockers' K.C.', who led and won the dockers' case in London in the first public wage arbitration award.

From then on, Bevin was for twenty years a power in the land as one of its chief trade union leaders; the mighty figure who made and led the gigantic Transport and General Workers Union; who broke the attempt to intervene in Russia against the Bolsheviks by threatening a transport strike; who led and lost the General Strike; and finally rose to be chairman of the T.U.C.

But the formative years were the obscure period from 1900 to 1920, before he became a big trade union 'boss'—twenty long years of struggle, of unaided decisions and steps in the dark, of serious responsibilities, and bitter defeats. Here are those 'hedgerows of experience'. Here he learned to train his instincts, to watch his step, to be both daring and cautious, to know and to use people, to persuade and to bargain. Above all, to bargain: for Bevin is the happy negotiator, as Churchill is the happy warrior. His mastery and delight in driving a bargain, in measuring the limits of bluffing and bullying that each side dare to go, in almost closing the door but not quite doing so, in judiciously mixing smooth and rough tactics, in never losing the advantage of having a clear conscience—all this he learned to perfection as an obscure young docker, staking his slender existence on untried experiments (trade unions were new then) and living perilously, always opposing superior powers.

From those days, also, stems his unshakable grip on working-class audiences, that confident familiarity which many years later enabled him easily to rout the 'intellectual' critics of his foreign policy at Labour Party Conferences, and to remain massively popular throughout a period of disappointments, bewilderment, and lean success.

It is very easy to list Mr Bevin's weaknesses as a Foreign Secretary. The chief of them lies in his handling of administrative jobs—such as Germany—where a negotiating technique does not apply (and where his officials are equally inexperienced). The next is in questions where his emotional prejudices intrude—such as Palestine and, again, Germany—

(particularly if his officials share his emotions, as they tend to in these cases). More obviously, he lacks the ordinary equipment for diplomacy—languages, historical studies, and a knowledge of foreigners and foreign nations.

His mind is powerful, but imprecise. He is supremely indiscreet and shockingly tactless. He will call the Americans 'moneylenders', and the French Foreign Minister a 'dear little man', in public; he will solemnly stake his reputation on 'solving' the Palestine problem in a moment of rashness, and will condescendingly pat a visiting Foreign Minister on the back in front of the newsreel camera. In fact, he makes every crude blunder which any conventional second-rate Foreign Secretary would avoid.

Also, he has made enemies in his own party, and has given them plenty to snigger over with his loud references to 'my policy', and his hackneyed complaint of being 'stabbed in the back'.

And yet, it is quite possible that history will rate him as one of the greatest Foreign Secretaries this country ever had, and the best she could possibly have had at this particular juncture. It is remarkable—indeed, it borders on the miraculous—how this lumbering Visigoth, with his habitual bragging and his countless minor *faux pas*, has never yet made a really big mistake (unless his Palestine policy will prove to have been one), and never yet taken a diametrically wrong course on major issues—such as his more sophisticated predecessors did at Munich or at Teheran—and has always been on the spot to 'grab with both hands' any real chance the moment it offered itself.

His manners may be rough, his mind may work clumsily, but his instinct is a precision instrument which stands him, and his country, in good stead. He has a smell for enemies, for dangers, for traps, where others, trained in easier schools, have to rely on eyesight. He has a truly marvellous gift for stalling, shamming dead, bluffing, for blandly landing a doubtful punch —and making it up afterwards. He has never been 'on easy street' but often 'in queer street', and his country is now profiting from this, as his class did before.

OBSERVER PROFILES

He was given charge of Britain's foreign affairs at a time charged with immense difficulties. The country was nearly bankrupt, physically exhausted, and sublimely innocent of its real circumstances. He found the British public in a somewhat low state of morale, doped by wartime emotions and quite willing to go on befuddling itself. He had to accept or dispel all kinds of smooth, half-baked expectations. He had no chance of playing to the gallery, no opportunity for spectacular tactical successes. He was obliged to play a waiting game, leaving the initiative to others and affecting a stout Palmerstonian self-confidence in far more dangerous circumstances than Palmerston ever faced. When historians compare Britain's position today with that of three years ago, they will not find that he has played that game badly.

The select, who live by their minds, rather than their instincts, easily get impatient and annoyed with Bevin. And, indeed, he has yet to prove that he can build success, as well as ward off disaster. Can he integrate Western Europe, carry the Commonwealth into a new amalgam, muddle his way back into the Middle East and get on better terms with America?

Intellectually, he has no answers; but in practice he might pull it off. In a curious way, Bevin always seems to get the last laugh on his opponents. There is something in him that makes mere cleverness look silly. Perhaps future generations may one day say that it was a particularly striking manifestation of the national genius that we had this man in this job at a time when everything depended on feeling, instinctively, who was for us and who against us.

MOLOTOV

IN the first fine, careless turmoil of the new Russia, the great men of the system were far from attaining that quasi-divinity which the iconoclastic West finds so tedious in them today.

They were thought of by their fellow-countrymen simply as human beings, with all the attributes of human beings everywhere, good and bad and even comic. They even had nicknames, now faded memories of the days of innocence locked in the hearts of careful Soviet citizens of middle age; and from these nicknames more may be learnt about the men who achieved them than from a whole volume of formal biography, pro or con. Stalin, for instance, had several—at least one of them highly expressive.

Mr Molotov, too, had a nickname, said to have been invented by the brilliant journalist and publicist, Karl Radek, who later atoned for it: Stone Bottom. It stuck because the supreme quality of Mr Molotov was, as it is today, his capacity for sitting at an office desk. It was far more expressive than Molotov, which means 'The Hammer'. This was his own choice of *nom-de-guerre* when, as the revolutionary young bourgeois, Vyacheslav Mihailovitch Scriabin—nephew of the composer—he abandoned the Civil Service future marked out for him by his father, and took instead to the Bolshevik underground.

Mr Molotov became a Bolshevik at the age of seventeen, not as a result of an unhappy childhood or any personal wrong but because revolt was in the air, and, if he was going to be a rebel, he proposed to become one in a cool, radical, uncompromising and businesslike way. He is certainly a good deal more of a hammer than he looks, but the Radek nickname fits him better. Others come and go, but Mr Molotov sits on. He was sitting firmly in Petrograd with all the strings of the local Bolshevik Party in his hands when Kamenev and Stalin came back from exile in Siberia after the March revolution to prepare the way for Lenin. He sat on through the wild and chaotic years of the intervention, the civil war, the famine. While Lenin, immensely his senior, saw him as a highly competent junior party official, and once called him 'the best filing-clerk in Russia', Stalin had already fixed on him as his born chief-of-staff.

And so Molotov went on sitting. He sat out the whole of Trotsky's impetuous career, which took some doing; for Trotsky, baulked in his frontal attack on Stalin, went bald-headed for Stalin's young men. Molotov sat, more firmly and patiently than ever, through the great purges and the trials—now as Prime Minister, or Chairman of the Council of People's Commissars, placed there by Stalin—still only General Secretary of the Party—as the best-qualified man in Russia to sit still and keep his head in difficult times and coolly impose a highly unpopular Party programme upon the official Government of the country.

He was still sitting in Moscow when Litvinov came back, defeated in his crusade for collective security, to be relegated to the limbo of lost causes. That was in May, 1939, and Mr Molotov became Commissar for Foreign Affairs and, enlarging his sphere of activity accordingly, proceeded with his self-appointed task of out-sitting the rest of the world.

Now, some years later, he is still at it. And it is easy to imagine the contempt, amused or irritated (for Mr Molotov carries an uncertain temper within the limitless framework of his patience), with which this man who has sat unshaken for thirty years at the very centre of one of the greatest earthquakes in history must regard the spasmodic attempts of his more volatile Western colleagues to make him budge.

Lenin was not the only man to underestimate the tenacity and character of this small, snub, pallid man in pince-nez, with his faint stammer, his faint bow, his fainter smile—and his terrible, his relentless devotion to Russia, to the Revolution, and to Stalin, whom, by his clear purpose and incorruptible fanaticism, he has done more than any other single man to uphold. The statesmen of the West also thought of him for too long as a colourless shadow, a mouthpiece, a sort of glorified clerk. If they had troubled to read a little in Soviet history they would have come to a different conclusion.

MOLOTOV

Mr Molotov is fifty-seven now. For thirty years he has been saying 'No'—No to all those in Russia (and their influence was sometimes almost overwhelming) who sought for a softening, an amelioration, a diversion, of Soviet official policy, laid down first by Lenin, then by Stalin. Thirty years ago, it is recorded, when Trotsky in committee made a particularly virulent attack on Stalin's protégé, who in all his youth and inexperience and vanity had been promoted over the heads of venerable fighters for the cause (Lenin was still alive), the young Molotov murmured back at him politely: 'Not everyone can be a genius, Comrade Trotsky; but we shall see who comes through in the end'.

Mr Molotov has always been a nervous man behind that studied, bleak exterior. Assumed by instinct even in those chaotic days in Petrograd in early 1917, when he worked decisively to keep the tiny Bolshevik party pure and uncontaminated by the broader, looser, more popular revolutionary parties which almost overwhelmed it, his constant rôle has been that of watch-dog of the Revolution. It is obviously very nervous work indeed, and Mr Molotov is just as obviously sometimes rattled. But he still goes on sitting.

He has another nickname now. Not in Russia, where he has long been above such things, but among the diplomats of Great Britain and America. They call him Aunty Moll. Even that is not as far-fetched as it sounds. It goes well enough with the pince-nez, the slightly fussy pedantry, the occasional unconcealed flusters. But above all it suggests the maiden aunt with a passion for the shipshape. And here, when it comes to it, is perhaps Mr Molotov's greatest service to Russia. In a country notorious for its untidiness, its fecklessness, its waywardness to the point of anarchy, Mr Molotov insists, for thirty years has insisted, that everything he has anything to do with must be just so. By sitting at his desk and keeping to the point of the moment until his opponents give way out of utter tedium he has ensured the downfall of his ablest rivals, and now, before all the world, occupies second place to Stalin alone.

ANDREI GROMYKO

M. GROMYKO is a man of medium height, with very dark eyes, a pale, sallow complexion, and thick black hair. His nose is prominent and his lower lip protrudes. He wears suits of black or grey, and uses horn-rimmed spectacles for reading. He speaks little, and has an air of intense concentration.

Andrei Gromyko is one of the most successful young men of the U.S.S.R., or, indeed, of the world. At the age of thirty-eight, as Soviet representative on the Security Council, he deals with the most senior diplomatists of the nations of the world.

Who his parents were cannot be exactly said. The Soviet Embassy regret they have no information about his father. His mother, they state, is working on the 'Gorodok' collective farm of the Svetilovichi district of the Gomel region of the Byelo-Russian Republic. In appearance, he might be the son of a Jewish skilled artisan.

Andrei was only nine at the time of the Russian revolution. He grew up during the first Five-Year Plan and, like most other able youths, was given a training as an engineer.

In 1938, at the age of thirty, he was taken into the Commissariat for Foreign Affairs in Moscow. After only one year's training he was sent out to Washington as Counsellor. He had never been abroad before and he spoke no English.

What impression America can have made on him can scarcely be imagined. Did he feel that he was being plunged into a strange, fabulous world—the ogre-haunted jungle of American capitalism? There is a sense, however, in which a Russian diplomat never leaves Russia; he still works within the familiar, secluded atmosphere of a Soviet office, with his duties clearly defined. Gromyko lived with his wife and two children in a Washington villa, much as he had lived in Moscow but more comfortably. He continued to play 'volley ball' for exercise and chess for recreation, to collect stamps and study endless reports, memoranda, and useful books. He did not mix with Americans at all and still remains, as an individual, practically unknown in Washington. His only first-hand contact with American life was a regular visit to the movies every Saturday afternoon.

ANDREI GROMYKO

Certainly his time in Washington was spent infinitely more strenuously than that of his opposite numbers in other Embassies. For example, he learnt English through books and the Embassy interpreter so accurately that today at conferences he frequently corrects the official translation on detailed points. Because of his method of learning, he speaks English laboriously, weighing and measuring each word.

After four years in Washington he was raised to be Chargé d'Affaires in May, 1943. Within three months he was raised again, this time to be Ambassador. He was still only thirty-five. How well-thought-of he must have been in Moscow, how trusted and proved sure, was shown even more remarkably when he was charged with representing the U.S.S.R. at the Dumbarton Oaks Conference the following autumn.

This marked a turning point and sharp change in his work. It was no longer a matter of working through official channels, hidden from the public eye, as he had done all his life. He now had to speak for his country in the floodlight of the world's attention. He had to debate publicly.

In some ways the impression he made was that of a badger coming into the unaccustomed light of day—tremendously strong, intelligent, and methodical, yet unable to see what was about him. He would attend conferences and then hurry back to the seclusion of his bureau, followed by his staff, to make reports and read instructions.

Whereas to the public outside Russia this performance may seem peculiar, maladroit, almost funny, Gromyko has undoubtedly impressed those who have had to deal with him as a formidable man in his way. A British observer at the London conference of U.N.O. noticed: 'Quite often, while others were speaking, he would sit with his eyes closed: but he was not relaxing; rather, concentrating and gathering his strength'. He would often emerge from a long silence with the bald statement 'That interpretation is not a right one'.

The important point about Andrei Gromyko is that he represents the new type of Russian diplomat, who is a product of the Soviet régime. He has been trained as an official, which is the opposite type of training from that of a revolutionary. His knowledge of life has been gained almost entirely within the U.S.S.R.

The contrast between him and the type of Soviet Ambassador of yesterday is almost complete. Men like Litvinov were trained as revolutionaries and were products of Western Europe, where they had lived in long exile. They easily understood other nations and were understandable to us. The Gromyko type neither understands us nor is understood by us: it simply functions, with great precision and skill, in obedience to orders.

As one watches Gromyko arriving in a large limousine at a conference hall, smooth, precise, unsmiling, dressed like the typical official of any country, it is hard to remember that he represents a country still suspicious because of its revolutionary past. As Russia's permanent representative on the Security Council, Gromyko is like the commander of an outpost in a strange country which *must* be perilous whatever appearances may suggest, because the inexorable logic of materialist history makes it so.

Whatever he may be like privately—few know, as he scarcely ever accepts invitations to unofficial meals—in public, Gromyko is always 'in uniform and on guard'; he is always the acutely single-minded servant of the Stalin régime, carrying out his orders with energetic accuracy, determined neither to neglect nor to exceed them by one iota.

If we are surprised at this rigid figure it is because we are still inclined to confuse Russian character with pre-revolutionary Russian literature, from Dostoevsky and Tchehov. There is no idealistic bohemianism about the young men trained in the Stalin school. They are dedicated to a life of discipline. When Gromyko says No; when he obstructs and objects and hair-splits; when he argues for hours, as he once did, whether a communiqué should read 'in due time' or 'in due course', he is not merely being cantankerous. He is thinking dutifully of Russia's security and anxiously of his orders from Moscow.

HECTOR McNEIL

HECTOR McNEIL'S appointment as Under-Secretary of State for Foreign Affairs was in some ways the most surprising of the junior appointments made after the Labour victory in 1945. This well-groomed burly young man, by birth a Clydeside worker and by training a journalist of the popular press, seemed altogether remote from diplomacy.

But he quickly made his impression both on Parliament and on the more pliant and unalterable audience in the Foreign Office. After little more than a year, Mr Attlee promoted him to be Minister of State.

Hector was born into a family of ship-builders at Garelochhead in 1910—a large working-class family of seven. His father and his grandfather were journeymen shipwrights, the type of men who made the Clyde famous throughout the world. Only a defect in one hand prevented young Hector from joining his father's trade as soon as he left school. The family opinion was that poor Hector would have to follow some clerical career, using his head to make a living.

So he made his way to Glasgow University. The great attraction there for him was the Union, where debates are conducted in the Parliamentary manner and where some of the ablest parliamentarians—such as Maxton and Elliot—had their first experience of debating. The forceful and commonsensical young McNeil did not fail to get himself listened to.

Still encouraged by his father to 'use his head', he joined the Glasgow branch of the Kemsley newspaper organisation. After six months he left, in 1932, to take a job with Lord Beaverbrook's Scottish office round the corner, sensing that the *Express* might offer him more scope. In the same year he was elected a Labour member of the Glasgow Town Council and married a charming wife. He was only twenty-two at that time and naturally was thrilled to find how rapidly life was opening up for him.

Beaverbrook visited Glasgow in 1935 and offered NcNeil a job on his London staff. So he came to the Capital at twenty-five and tasted the Beaverbrook distillation of political High

Life that so many able young men of Left opinions have tasted before and after him. Among Lord Beaverbrook's circle of friends at that time were such colourful characters as Aneurin Bevan, Randolph Churchill, and such like. It was all great fun, but the deliberate and practical Hector did not entirely fit into their milieu. He returned to Glasgow in 1937 to become night news editor of the *Scottish Daily Express*, and to continue in local politics, for he had not resigned from the Glasgow Town Council. As a councillor McNeil interested himself in Committees dealing with sanitation, health, and public libraries. He seldom spoke at Council meetings and in 1938 resigned as his work for the *Express* became too time-consuming and took him too frequently to London.

He was on the *Evening Standard* during the first years of the war. In 1941 he had a chance to stand for Parliament and was returned unopposed as the Labour Member for Greenock. That he made no special impression at Westminster on arrival is not surprising: in '41 the House was concerned with more momentous matters than the arrival of new Members.

McNeil did not join the few 'oppositional' Labour members (and therefore, like most of his superiors, cannot show evidence of having foreseen any unfortunate consequences of the Churchill-Eden foreign policy), but followed the line of those adhering to the Coalition. A year later he was 'in office' in the modest position of Parliamentary Private Secretary to Mr Philip Noel-Baker, then Parliamentary Secretary to the Minister of War Transport. No one can be associated with Mr Philip Noel-Baker without acquiring at least an interest in and some factual knowledge of foreign affairs.

Hector McNeil now finds himself, at thirty-eight, a fairly prominent figure in world affairs and the youngest Privy Councillor of the United Kingdom. His job is nothing less than that of representing his country at those international conferences which the Foreign Secretary does not himself attend or, alternately, of speaking for His Majesty's Government in Parliament on foreign affairs in his chief's absence. He also has been specially commissioned to consider what changes should

HECTOR MCNEIL

be made in the organisation and staffing of the Diplomatic Service—a fairly tall order for so new a comer, but one he is likely to carry out more boldly than would the type of politician brought up to venerate all diplomats.

In Parliament he has already established his reputation as a clear, fearless, and effective speaker. It is no easy matter to answer extempore adjournment debates, which McNeil has had to do more often than any other Minister in the present Government. As an individual, Hector McNeil is definitely likeable. His Clydeside electors like him: he has remained culturally one of them. Whereas Aneurin Bevan, for example, uses peculiar modern words (such as 'purposive' for 'purposeful')—Hector McNeil's diction has remained substantially unaltered. His favourite outing is still to watch soccer.

The highbrows, among whom he now does his daily work, like him too. They have found that behind his slow, deliberate Scottish speech and steady gaze there is an active and receptive brain. And he has character, without subtle shades of colour maybe, but with some native strength.

Perhaps the most promising sign he has shown of real calibre is that his translation from provincial journalist to minor statesman has not unduly impressed him. McNeil has remained accessible, plain in manner and no more nor less self-confident than he was before his elevation.

Hector McNeil has the ability to express himself, to take responsibility and give decisions which are the essentials in politics. Whether he has the originality, moral force, and touch of brilliance needed to make a great statesman it would be unwise to pronounce upon. It is already much that a man holding responsibility, if only secondary, in foreign affairs at a time like the present has made a solid success of his job.

That Britain is represented at Peace Conferences by two men of plain working-class origin, Bevin and McNeil, while the Soviet spokesmen, Molotov and Vyshinsky, are highly educated persons of bourgeois parentage is one of those little facts which tend to be obscured by propaganda but which are indicative of a reality in the modern world.

COUNT SFORZA

IN his seventy-fifth year, Count Sforza, the Italian Foreign Minister, after a quarter of a century's pause, rejoined European diplomacy at the Paris Conference on the Marshall Plan in July, 1947. Of those present in the gilded dining hall at the Quai d'Orsay, hardly anyone else could have remembered the time when he had last adorned, and sometimes dominated, gatherings like this. Tall, bearded, monocled, immensely dignified, perfectly dressed, the old statesman looked like a figure from another age—a fitting opposite number to Sir Edward Grey rather than Mr Ernest Bevin. He spoke—and here was an old master practising an almost defunct craft, grand diplomatic oratory with every word thrice sifted, and political allusion carefully balanced against literary effect. He was the only speaker to make the Assembly applaud.

His return is the climax of a political life which, after the brightest promise, had seemed to fade out in tragic frustration. Up to the advent of Mussolini, Sforza's career is all splendour and success; afterwards, all defeat and denial—till this late, almost unhoped-for personal triumph and vindication.

Sforza's youth and rise belong to a now almost legendary past—the days before 1914, the golden autumn of the old Europe. He combined breeding, wealth, looks, charm, brains, and brilliance. The world spread out before him. Constantinople, Peking, Paris, Madrid, London were the stations of a smooth and distinguished diplomatic career. In 1919 he became Under-Secretary of State; in 1920, Foreign Minister.

The years 1920 to 1922 were an exciting period. The war leaders passed from the scene. There was a new cast—Bonar Law, Briand, Rathenau—and a new outlook, a brave and early attempt to make peace real; but it led to nothing. Count Sforza was perhaps the most brilliant, certainly the most active of the new statesmen of Europe. He crowded great activity into his short tenure of office; he shone at the Supreme Allied Council and the League of Nations; above all, he gave Italian foreign policy a clear and intelligible direction, such as it has never had since, and hardly before. It is easy to feel one's grievances, it is harder to see one's opportunities. While Fascists and Nationalists already groaned about Italy's disappointed ambitions, Sforza maintained that the Versailles settlement had given Italy her supreme chance. 'Italy's position', he used to say, 'is what France's position would be if Germany had suddenly vanished from the map.'

The overpowering neighbour and eternal nightmare of Italy, the Austro-Hungarian Empire, had gone, leaving in its place small and new countries. In this situation, what did petty territorial ambitions matter! All Italy had to do now was to be generous, tactful, constructive, to become, almost inevitably, the leader and rallying-point of all Central and South-Eastern Europe. Sforza concluded pacts with Czechoslovakia and Rumania, he called a Conference of the succession States in Rome. He liquidated d'Annunzio's Fiume adventure, and turned a virtual state of war with Yugoslavia into friendship with the treaty of Rapallo, which he concluded in November, 1920. It was his greatest triumph, and it won him the highest Italian distinction, the Collar of the Annunziata, which made him a 'Cousin of the King'.

At the same time, it became the cause of his downfall. A secret clause in the treaty, withheld from the Italian Parliament at ratification-time, ceded a little port near Fiume to Yugoslavia. The nationalist outcry at the revelation overthrew the Government, and led indirectly, after a short interval, to Mussolini's march on Rome.

When Mussolini took power, Sforza was Italian Ambassador in Paris. He sent in his resignation firmly, clearly, and at once, and returned to Italy to fight. Used to success, he hardly expected defeat at the hands of an amateurish ruffian. He rallied the opposition to Fascism in the Senate. He led it, bravely in the face of mounting personal dangers, for some years. It is hard to say when he realised that he was fighting a losing battle. In 1927, at any rate, he transferred his fighting post to France, still carefully and demonstratively staying near the Italian frontier. It was still fight, not flight. All the time Count Sforza felt still a dignitary and servant of Italy in exile, and in a sense he was; for as a titular 'Cousin of the King' he retained the lifelong right to tender advice to the Crown, and in one case he availed himself of this right. In May, 1940, he addressed a memorandum to King Victor Emmanuel, warning him in grave terms against the 'folly' of declaring war on Britain and France. He received no answer; and it seems that it was this final slight that turned him from a lifelong Monarchist into a Republican.

Then came flight from France, and exile in America. He remained a big figure among 'Free Italians' abroad, but there is no denying that by now an air of unreality had settled on his political activities. A man of about seventy, twenty years out of office, fifteen years out of his country, but still gravely talking and acting as if in some way he were the real Foreign Minister of his country and everything else were forgery and usurpation: people would shake their heads and smile sadly.

Mussolini fell, but this no longer automatically made Sforza rise. Instead misfortune deepened. Sforza abroad had at any rate been a name and a symbol. Returning home to his shattered and embattled country under Allied auspices, he was a mere individual, out of touch, without party or following, half-committed to alien policies, and easily put in a false position. Had his life ended in 1944 or 1945 it would have seemed unmitigated tragedy, providing almost a cautionary tale. People would have held him up as the warning example of a brilliant statesman who ruined himself, his work, his career, his cause, everything, by choosing exile and cutting his links with his country.

And now, what has become of that cautionary tale? There is triumph at last, all the sweeter for being so over-long in coming. Mussolini dead and his memory cursed; Italy a Republic; and Count Sforza her Foreign Minister again—able to lead her back into the comity of nations, able to put once more at her service his insight, his finesse, a still undimmed vision, and a hand that has not lost its cunning. Is it not almost 1920 over again? With all the obvious differences, there is again that postwar sense of new faces and a new and brave start, of new hopes amidst desolation, of peace to be made real; a dreamlike feeling, perhaps, of *déjà vu*; but also the elation of a second chance. If at first sight this old aristocrat seems a man from the past and a stranger on the diplomatic scene of our day—in truth it is perhaps the others who are the strangers, and he alone is at home on this particular scene. He has seen it all before. He re-enters it, with dignified mastery and a secret delight, a grand old actor who at last, at last, is given the rôle of his life.

GREAT POWERS

JOSEPH STALIN

THE Soviet leader is ageing. Those who have seen him in the Kremlin quite recently say that he looks perhaps ten years older than he is. His yellowish, pock-marked face, all in thick folds and thin wrinkles, with heavy reddish rings under the eyes, has an unhealthy look. He gives the impression of premature oldness and dogged fatigue.

Stalin's life has been a truly amazing succession of revolution in 1905, obscurity, revolution again in 1917, and internal authority growing to totality, world-shaking conflict, and war diplomacy. Fifty years of Parliamentary life in any Western country are less exhausting than five years of a career like this.

Surrounded by the splendours of his unique position as a State-builder and warrior, by the ghosts of his rivals and victimised comrades, by the life-noise of the Eurasian double continent, to the moulding of which he has contributed so much, and by the appalling ruins of war-ravaged Russia, he is seen by many as Cromwell-cum-Peter the Great impersonated in a modern Socialist.

After nearly half a century of moving on the edges of History's precipices, he still goes on climbing. His infrequent visitors are impressed by the evidence not only of his ageing but also of his obvious mastery of all the multiple and complex State affairs, by his clear-headedness, practical sense, and calm self-confidence. Like no other modern statesman he has grown to an awe-inspiring, almost mythical stature. Yet he has remained the most prosaic of all of them. This contrast between qualities both awe-inspiring and prosaic—one is tempted to say mediocre—is perhaps the most puzzling thing about him.

His loneliness and remoteness from his own people are perhaps greater today than ever before. Twenty years ago he was still the relatively obscure and accessible Secretary-General of the Party. Gradually he became respected by many, feared by everybody and loved almost by nobody. Only since recent days of victory has warmth appeared in the feelings of the ordinary Russian towards him. But even now that feeling lacks intimacy —there has been more gratitude for victory than real affection shown.

He has built and climbed the massive pyramid of power only to find himself completely alone at its summit. The slopes of the pyramid are strewn with the bodies of the old Bolshevik Guard, the political body in which he himself had grown and matured—and to which he himself still belongs as the sole survivor. There are few personal human links between him and the younger Party leaders and Army officers who obey his orders and whom he shifts up and down the Soviet hierarchical ladders as he pleases. So few, indeed, are those links that he has not yet been able to point to any among his lieutenants as his trusted successor.

His leadership is not that of a teacher followed by disciples. He is the super-specialist in the technique of power, with all the buttons and knobs of a vast power-machine at his finger tips. For years he has been working this machine, a thing of his own creation, with unerring sureness of touch. It is no wonder that he has not been able to single out any of its buttons as his spiritual heir.

The aftermath of the war has, for Stalin, been a time of great dilemmas in statecraft. His recent policy has been a vague, perhaps involuntary, drifting away from his previous simple line of isolation. Not that he has decided to resume Trotsky's fight against world-capitalism for ideological motives, out of loyalty to the workers of the world. Far from it. Rather the fact has been that Russia's own condition since the war has been such as to make Communism in one country—the programme of ideological and economic isolation—unreal. Two or three years ago he must have reached the conclusion that the experiment of a planned economy had to be carried at least into the neighbouring countries, so that Russia should recover from the blows of the war.

Recently Stalin confided his view of the future to a Central European visitor.

A planned economy in Russia and the countries of Eastern and Central Europe [he said] will enable us to heal our wounds much quicker and less painfully than we could do otherwise. If the capitalist world leaves us in peace and allows us to go on planning and building for twenty or thirty years in the vast area from the Pacific to the Oder and the Adriatic we shall eventually reach such a high standard of living that, without wars or bloody revolutions, the rest of the world will follow our Communist example.

This does not sound like world revolution in the style of Lenin and Trotsky. It does not sound like the 'Socialism in one country', which was the 1923–43 phase of Stalinism. The new expansionist Stalin policy has aroused much fresh suspicion and hostility in the West. Confronted with this hostility Stalin's mind is apparently vacillating between 'From the Pacific to the Oder and the Adriatic' and his earlier tenet of 'Socialism in one country'.

At home his chief preoccupation is the revival of the Party and the restoration of its influence over the people. In the war years he appealed to Nationalist rather than to Communist sentiment. He also made the Party into the Army's junior partner. He had little time to watch the internal affairs of the Party.

After the war the Russian domestic scene must have given him a rude shock and filled him with apprehension. The wave of Nationalism sweeping the country threatened to swamp all that had remained of its Communist consciousness. The Army had become dangerously accustomed to having the Party at its feet. A mood of cynicism and indifference to Party matters was invading Soviet life. The old Secretary-General of the Party re-awakened in the Generalissimo. The country clearly needed a political shake-up; and something like a campaign of Communist revivalism was initiated from the Kremlin.

JOSEPH STALIN

At times it looks as if the Soviet leader might be dimly aware of his limitations. He may look back with nostalgia to the distant days of his youth when he was a clandestine agitator for revolution in the land of the Tsars. In any case, he has decided to include his very early Socialist writings in the newly published volumes of his utterances. They are not the work of genius. They are not even the work of a really gifted agitator. But in their straight-forwardness of purpose they are much superior to the canonised preachings of his later years. If he should now be looking back to his own modest beginnings one might paraphrase Burke's aphorism on Cromwell. One might say that in Stalin ambition and lust of power had not wholly suppressed, but only suspended, his humanly Socialist sentiment.

KING IBN SAUD

IBN SAUD is the world's most notable example of a self-made man. Starting empty-handed, he has in his lifetime conquered and organised the great Arabian kingdom to which he has given his family name.

His forbears of the House of Saud conquered Arabia in the eighteenth century as the strong arm of a puritan crusade preached by the religious reformer, Abdul Wahhab. Hence the nickname Wahhabite, which is sometimes given to the Saudi dynasty. In the nineteenth century they lost all their gains at the hands, first of Egypt and then of the rival Arabian family of Rashid. Ibn Saud, who was born in 1880, therefore spent his youth as a landless refugee at the Court of Koweit, on the Persian Gulf.

In 1901 he brought off the stroke of genius that was the start of his great career. Thanks to good intelligence, swift riding, and surprise, he was able in a night to penetrate and win back from the Rashids the town of Riadh, capital of Nejd and of the ancestral lands of his family. So began the gradual and steady gain of territory which he has never since lost.

Like every Arabian empire-builder from Mahomet down, he derives his generating force from his religious enthusiasm. He combines with it great practical qualities. With a vision remarkable in one who had never been outside nomad Arabia, he saw that the surest future lay in settling the Beduin on the land, and curing their customs of movement and feud. Probably the most fundamental of his many reforms was the inauguration in 1910 of the part religious, part military, and part agricultural brotherhoods which he has settled in colonies all over the country, and to which he gives religious and agricultural teaching in return for certain military services.

By June, 1914, he had conquered territory up to the Persian Gulf, and that perspicacious traveller, Miss Gertrude Bell, was reporting that 'Ibn Saud is now the chief figure in Central Arabia'. But the War Cabinet of 1915 did not plump for her advice. When it began to plan the famous Arab revolt against the Turks, it tied two strings to its bow. The India Office, working westward from the Persian Gulf, sent Captain Shakespear to Ibn Saud of Nejd. The Foreign Office, working eastward from the Red Sea, sent T. E. Lawrence to King Hussein of the Hedjaz, Sharif of Mecca.

The accidental bullet which killed Captain Shakespear in a tribal skirmish helped to decide London in favour of Lawrence's man. The large sum of £200,000 monthly, paid in gold, was handed to King Hussein, whereas Ibn Saud's neutrality was purchased at the smaller fee of £5,000 a month. The Arab revolt was successful, but the long run was to prove that the Foreign Office had backed its weaker champion. By 1925 Ibn Saud had attacked and conquered the neighbouring Hedjaz. Hussein had fled and the Saudis were rulers of Mecca.

Inland, Nejd had presented him with internal problems only. The Hedjaz and Mecca, to which the faithful from all over Islam make annual pilgrimage, brought him international complications. Many Moslems were averse to Wahhabism and regarded his seizure of Mecca as impious. It took all his diplomacy and capacity for living things down to convince his coreligionists that he was a satisfactory trustee for their Holy Places.

Though the two territories of Hedjaz and Nejd are today one kingdom, the difference between them is still marked by differing constitutions. In Nejd, the patriarchal power of the Sauds is absolute. It is administered by the king's eldest son, the Emir Saud. The Hedjaz is by contrast governed through a local Council of State. The son who administers it, the Emir Feisal, is also the King's Foreign Minister. Others of the score of sons born to him by his four wives fulfil lesser offices.

What are the binding forces whereby Ibn Saud has in four decades united tribes once so quarrelsome and parochial? One is his devout way of life and religious leadership. Another is the religious toleration without which no Arab Empire has ever survived the first fine flush of establishment. A third is his physical stamina and capacity for hard work. He is six feet four inches tall. Though, today, he walks slightly stiffly as the result of old wounds, he is still regarded as a lusty fighter. His working day would tire anyone of less powerful physique. Another asset is his simplicity. His throne room is an office where any tribesman, however humble, may call and address him by his first name—Abdul Aziz, Servant of the Mighty One.

But perhaps the most potent of all his qualities is the breadth of mind which gives him patience to let developments take their time, and which endows him with a capacity for compromise that is unusual in his race. These gifts make him a good diplomat. They have also enabled him to bring in western innovations without offending the puritanism of his Wahhabi followers. He rejects only such inventions as are contrary to his religion; anything else he is ready to introduce as fast as he can accustom his people to it. He was a great man long before the American and British oil prospectors of the 1930s revealed that his kingdom is one of the richest oil bearing areas in the world.

He is an old friend of Britain. His treaties with her have been cemented by many mutual friendships with Englishmen. His admiration for them and their country never flinched during the dark days of the loss of Somaliland, the Iraqi revolt, and Rommel's advance to Alamein. The British Empire never had a more shrewd or more staunch Arab friend.

Further, he is a wise counsellor to the Arab world. Behind the security of his forbidding frontiers, he has developed a longer vision and a more balanced view of nationalism than some of the other Arab States. As an older man than most of his fellow rulers, he is in a position to give advice. History suggests that if the Arab unity movement is to become strong, it must develop a religious background. If so, it may in the end owe no more to the modern gadgets—press, radio transmitters, and air lines—owned and operated by Egypt or Iraq than to Ibn Saud's austerity, deliberative ways, and moral strength.

One parting snapshot: 'What vitality, Charles, in one getting on for seventy', said Mr Churchill to Lord Moran, as he rose from the King's side after their meeting in February, 1945. King Ibn Saud will relish that remark. Applause from experts is applause indeed.

JAWAHARLAL NEHRU

THE gifted and implacable man who has stood second in the Nationalist uprising of India enters his sixtieth year in 1948. He was the pivotal figure of Lord Wavell's decisive political manoeuvres during 1946–47. In any country or society his distinction would be undeniable. He is personally irresistible, being slight, keen, and of quiet manner. He looks well in clothes of any pattern. At Westminster there are, perhaps, not more than twenty men whose spoken English is equal to his in purity. His autobiography proclaims his mastery of the pen in a language to which he was not born.

His family is Kashmiri Brahmin, long resident in the central city of Allahabad. His father, Motilal Nehru, was a man of unusual quality—eminent in the law, a born councillor, wholly European in outlook and daily life, and yet latterly a supporter of Gandhi's civil disobedience. (The legal-academic title Pundit is rightly attached to both. The irrational Hunterian spelling of Indian names and titles has misled the English-speaking world into rhyming it with Bandit.)

Jawaharlal Nehru was sent to Harrow and on to Trinity, Cambridge. At both places he was happy, and he emerged a Westerner in habit, thought, and interests. Returning to India thirty-five years ago, he was slow to find himself. He had no liking for the law and knew next to nothing of his own people. He was aroused, transformed, by the storms of 1919–20, beginning with the Amritsar tragedy and the first Gandhi crusade of civil disobedience. The young Nehru was serving his initial prison sentence when Gandhi entered an Indian jail for the first time. Thenceforward the pair were inseparable. Nehru, who was to be several times President of the National Congress, submitted to the Mahatma's dictatorship. During more than twenty years he was unable to break away. It was Nehru who, in 1928, succeeded in changing the keyword of Indian nationalism from *Swaraj* (Own rule) to Independence.

In the public life of our time there was no partnership more significant than that of these two, and certainly none more singular. They united upon one political idea alone—complete freedom for India. In everything else they were opposites. Gandhi was an antique Hindu, an Indian villager, a rebel against the modern age—rejecting science, industry, organisation, governance. He demanded a return to the barest peasant mode of living. Standing immovably on the doctrine of non-violence, he expressed a religious mysticism that was entirely his own.

Nehru is an impassioned modern. His reading is English and French. He rejoices in the intellectual riches of the West. He is a thorough-going rationalist. The spectacle of Hinduism, or of religion anywhere as a system, fills him with horror. He is a Socialist, deeply influenced by Moscow. His vision of the future India is Leninist. He wants industrialisation, hydroelectric power, great-scale agriculture. In his intellectual world Gandhism is nonsense, while protest fasting is a fantastic irrelevance. Yet he believed all along that the cause of Indian freedom, the single motive of his own life, could not be furthered unless Gandhi's ascendancy was upheld so long as he remained in the field.

The soul of this emancipated Hindu is a battle-ground. 'I have become', he writes, 'a queer mixture of East and West, out of place everywhere, at home nowhere.' The spiritual antagonism between himself and Gandhi covers only part of a complex self-contradiction. Nehru knows that the Socialism he demands is alien from the mass of Indian nationalists. He describes himself as a repentant bourgeois, and the National Congress is a bourgeois body. Its membership is middle-class; its funds come mainly from wealthy Hindus. Gandhi himself, arch-enemy of power-industry, always defended the big landlords. Nehru is the one Congress leader who is fully aware of the truth that political change in India must be the prelude to a vast social upheaval, involving the entire structure of caste and land, family and group, authority and law.

He has never had any tolerance for constitutional advance or political effort. His position in the Nationalist movement is no less paradoxical than his relation to Gandhi. Reform Acts were odious to him. Never himself a candidate, he refused to touch the Legislatures, although he is the most effective of election campaigners. His tours have been not unlike those of a W. J. Bryan or an early Lloyd George. As a young agrarian agitator he followed Gandhi into the villages, discovered his own talent, and tasted the intoxication of mass meetings. By instinct an authoritarian, he holds an attitude towards the multitude, which is the opposite of Gandhi's. He loathes demonstrations; processions move him to scorn. He confesses to a 'wholly undemocratic distaste for elections'. The atmosphere of Congress politics was abhorrent to him, and more than once he escaped to England and Europe for the sake of fresh air and mental stimulus. The Cripps Mission of 1942 gave him his first experience of negotiation with equals (he is a friend of Sir Stafford's) and, to do him justice, he displayed a fine reasonableness as the crisis developed. He was against the breaking-off.

He adhered to non-co-operation and the boycott, but his creed had no place for non-resistance. His hatred of military aggression is unbounded. None the less he was the most dangerous man in India when the Japanese were hammering at the gate. 'We cannot', he declared, 'participate in Britain's war effort.' Or, again, 'Come what may, we will come out as a free nation or be thrown into the ashes.'

In and out of prison frequently after middle life, Nehru was arrested in August, 1942, after Gandhi, on behalf of the Congress Party, had proclaimed 'open rebellion'. A simple declaration calling off civil disobedience would have sufficed to open the door for themselves and hundreds of lesser political prisoners. They preferred to maintain the formula, which, of necessity, was meaningless in wartime. The Bengal famine of 1943 furnished a hard test of their attitude and method. Men of the deepest compassion, both of them, Gandhi and Nehru could not bring themselves to answer the appeal of their countrymen for co-operation with the British Government during the silent agony of that year. In the presence of a calamity unequalled for severity in the India of our time, their united and whole-hearted service would have been a benediction without measure. But the negative dogma held them in its grip.

OBSERVER PROFILES

Although Jawaharlal Nehru, a persistent agitator and crusader, held himself aloof from all forms of governing responsibility until the British decision had been made, and was thus wholly without administrative experience, he was the one possible head of the first National Government. He was never interested in either the programme or the theory of dominion status; it was he who, in the Constituent Assembly, moved the Congress resolution for an independent Indian Republic. His ordeal of preparation had been searching and prolonged. Few popular leaders have endured more punishment or displayed a firmer consistency. Inevitably he was Prime Minister at Delhi when the governing authority was transferred in August, 1947; and there cannot be many among his opponents who would wish to deny that in the opening crisis of Indian freedom, stained by the appalling massacres in the Punjab, Nehru displayed high qualities of statesmanship—among them resolution, humanity, and clearness of mind. Needless to say, he was the central figure at Gandhi's funeral. Knowing well, as he faced that indescribable multitude, that his triumph had been made possible through the sustained power of the Mahatma alone, he delivered a brief and restrained eulogy. It was a model of eloquence, couched in the simplest English words.

GENERAL FRANCO

WHEN the Captain of the Moorish Infantry, Don Francisco Franco y Bahamonde, was informed that he would not be promoted to the rank of major, in spite of his merits in the field, because a young man of twenty-five could not be a major, he rebelled and demanded his deserts from the King of Spain. His elders and superiors were given the lie; Franco became the youngest major in the Spanish Army, hated, envied, and distrusted accordingly. He was more alone than he had been in the military academy where he had escaped from unpopularity and ridicule into grim, successful study.

Major Franco was sent to Oviedo, to rot in the garrison, waiting in vain for his allotted battalion. He volunteered for the *Tercio*, the Foreign Legion which had just been founded to serve as a shock-troop in the smouldering Moroccan war, fighting side by side with the savage Moors. Franco, later to be welcomed elsewhere as a Great Christian Gentleman, became the most successful and ruthless organiser and leader of the Legionaries, who were more savage even than the Moors of the *Regulares*.

Separated by his rank and inhuman earnestness from the officers of his own age, isolated by his youth and single-minded ambition from those of his own rank, the *Comandantin*—the 'Little Major', as they called him—studied military science and staked his life (for he is as brave as callous) to prove them all wrong. War was his medium and his only contact with life. He had no friends, but he was feared and left alone.

His curious luck inspired awe and distrust: when the founder of the Legion, Millan Astray, resigned the command because of his crippling wounds, Franco succeeded him—after the death in battle of his two higher ranking competitors. He was C.O. of the Legion when Spain's paternally blundering dictator, Primo de Rivera, decided to give up Morocco and the disastrous, costly, unpopular war for its conquest. Against this decision Franco rebelled at Ben Tieb, showing the old General, by a symbolic act of calculated rudeness, how strongly he felt. The Dictator put the operations into the hands of Colonel

Franco; the Moroccan War was fought to its end, and Franco, aged thirty-four became General.

There was no longer a war in which a lonely, chubby, earnest young man could prove his strength. Franco became Director of the Military Academy. He turned himself into a theoretician, based on the German and French schools of exact military science, and he spoke to his pupils of that science and of the lost Spanish Empire to be reconquered, while the Spanish monarchy was breaking up. At that time he went to Saint-Cyr and sat at the feet of Marshal Pétain.

A year later, in 1931, he swore the oath of loyalty to the Republic. The Court, which at one time had supported him, had not proved the right field for his bleak ambition. But when the young Republic began to cut down the number of officers, regarding them as a costly and dangerous luxury for a democracy which did not want an empire, many of the innumerable generals began to conspire more or less openly. Franco kept sagely in the background, although no one was more deeply hit in the very core of his convictions than this man, to whom an army made for war was the only satisfactory social form, his only mode of self-expression. And the Republic kept him in important posts.

Then Franco, a taciturn rebel against an anti-militarist democratic State, grew into a politician. Not for nothing was he imbued with the severe military logic of Clausewitz, to whom war is a continuation of politics by different means; he, Franco, had to turn politics into a war by different means. The ordered hierarchy of the Army would be put in its rightful place. The social structure would be based on discipline and the hierarchical principle. The threatening 'disorder' with its many names, Democracy, Liberalism, Communism, Socialism, Anarchism, would be stamped out.

The pale-faced, fat little soldier, with sluggish nervous reactions and without human sympathy, felt the vocation to be the leader, the Caudillo, of the perfect soldier's State. He had ordered undisciplined soldiers to be shot without compunction. Why should he have compunction at shooting or hanging rebels? For all those who stood in the way of his ideal order were rebels against the Army and against its future Empire.

Franco was the Chief of Staff of the rebellion against the Spanish Republic which broke out in all the garrisons in July, 1936. He became its Generalissimo by his own act and by the good luck which once more cleared his path. Calvo Sotelo, the presumptive dictator, was killed before the actual rising, the Generals Sanjurjo and Mola died in accidents. Franco was left undisputed leader.

He accepted as his due the help from the Fascist and National-Socialist Powers, because he was convinced that they stood for his aims in his own country: hierarchical order, and the fight against 'Liberalism' and all its offsprings, lumped together as 'Communism'.

This conviction never changed in the new stage of the long war, whatever the pitch of Franco's public speeches. He had to help and back his own kind. Threats and compliments cannot reach him, immured as he is in his self-belief and rigid vision of the world. His instruments of power, Falange and the Army, may splinter and break; his German and Italian backers—from whom he kept sagely aloof in their struggle for world domination as well as in their struggle for life—may have fallen; Europe may rally for something called freedom, or it may fall a prey to advancing Communist revolution: General Franco has to stand and fight for his authoritarian world—or vanish.

WESTMINSTER GALLERY

SIR STAFFORD CRIPPS

'WHEN you grow up', wrote Theresa Cripps, Stafford's mother, 'you will find heaps and heaps of work of every sort and kind waiting to be done, and never imagine that God has not given you the power to take your share in helping the world to better and nobler things.'

The words were written to her eldest son, but they might have been addressed to Stafford, the youngest. His career, the ordinary man would feel, has been modelled on them—a life of asceticism devoted to the good of the unfortunate. This remarkable woman also wrote of her children: 'I should like their living to be of the simplest, without reference to show and other follies. I should like them to be trained to be undogmatic and unsectarian Christians, charitable to all churches and sects, studying the precepts and actions of Christ as their example, taking their religious inspiration directly from the spirit of the New Testament. . . .'

Has not Elijah fulfilled the prophecy? Has he not lived without show 'and other follies'? Has he not been charitable to all sects? Has he not loved the New Testament and lived only for the poor? And now, as in a simple story book, virtue is having its reward. The wilderness is left behind; beyond is the Temple, which has somehow turned up in the vicinity of 10 Downing Street.

A beautiful story, but it projects a figure that is a little too simple for reality. Nobody is quite so simple as that, least of all Sir Stafford Cripps. He is a Christian without theology and a Socialist without Marxist doctrine. He is a scientist turned lawyer and a lawyer turned politician. He is a man who believes in the Christian virtue of love and charity, and yet is one of the few politicians who have no personal claque. 'He hardly gives one the chance to love him', one of his closest associates remarks.

SIR STAFFORD CRIPPS

He is an ascetic, apparently indifferent to the world, and yet far up the ladder of power. He is an eccentric who is not a Bohemian. The paradoxes are so endless and baffling that every easy interpretation of this self-sufficient man, moving icily through the warm corrupting atmosphere of politics, breaks off and comes to nothing. And yet somehow the contradictions must be resolved.

Sir Stafford's career can conveniently be divided into three phases. The first would be his youth and early manhood—riding, fishing and shooting, but especially riding. 'Yesterday', he wrote to his father, 'I had a race with Mr Elwell. It was awful fun; we fair galloped for all we could go, and Nipper (whom you must thank Uncle for) beat Eighteen by two and a half lengths, and I could hardly pull him up for about 150 yards.' Warm, gay words, warmer and gayer than any he has written since.

At Winchester he specialised in science, and after he had won a science scholarship to New College, he was invited by Sir William Ramsay, the great chemist, to join his research staff at University College. His decision to switch over to the Bar is a little surprising, but understandable when one remembers that both his father and grandfather were distinguished lawyers.

So far, in fact, the pattern of his life is almost conventional; a hundred other young men of his class and attainments might have followed the same course. Even the decision to join Labour is not really an abrupt departure, given Stafford's religious convictions. Christianity, he once thought, could save the world, the lion would be persuaded to turn vegetarian and lie down with the lamb, and man, at long last, would cease to slay his brother. But once he felt that the churches could not translate these beliefs into practice, his conversion to Socialism was a logical step: the pattern is not really disturbed.

Phase Two would open somewhere about 1932, when the Socialist League was formed and Cripps became its chairman a few months later. It might be summed up as the revolutionary stage of his career, but a better way of seeing it is as a test of him as a leader of men. At no time perhaps was the Labour Movement in greater need. The party had been deserted by MacDonald and Snowden, but the League's policy, with its talk of emergency powers and abolition of the House of Lords, was hardly calculated to win the approval of the hierarchy, shaken by catastrophic defeat.

The Conservatives, on the other hand, were delighted. *The Times* sourly agreed with 'a prominent member of the party', who is supposed to have said that Cripps lost the Movement '20,000 votes every time he... opened his mouth'. The *Morning Post* was in fine form. 'Sir Stafford Cripps', it wrote, 'known abroad as Sir Scrapps, among his friends as Scrappy, and among the ungrateful proletariat as Cripes....' Even the *Manchester Guardian* could say that 'Sir Stafford Cripps, if he continues, is more likely to be the architect of a British Fascism, based on the fears of a frightened middle class, than Sir Oswald Mosley.'

More serious was the reaction of the Labour Movement as a whole. The League began with the aim of injecting a militant Socialism into the party and afterwards became the spearhead of the demand for the United Front. But as time went on the campaign was less of a call for unity than an undignified quarrel between Cripps and the orthodox leaders.

Phase Three is the happier period of the last few years—his mission to India and his outstanding success at both the Ministry of Aircraft Production and the Board of Trade. Even his keenest political opponents gladly admit the range, speed, and certainty with which Cripps's mind works on a host of various and tangled problems. Certainly he is a great administrator and executive. Has something deeper and broader emerged since the days of the Socialist League? For as his star rises, and others pale and gutter out, it is natural that people should sometimes think of him as a future Premier.

Surely here is Elijah at last, to lead us through the sandy wastes of austerity. Only one thing would seem to be lacking among these many talents. 'He is not at home', Fenner Brockway noticed, 'among the working class, and workers do not feel at their ease with him.' And, after all, there can be only three explanations of that. It may be that Stafford really is the Saint strayed into politics, and that we average sensual men feel embarrassed in his presence. But it could also be due to an inner pride, invincible and unyielding under the hair-shirt. Or to the familiar and wearisome desire for power. Perhaps if Stafford could for once say: 'I don't know the answer', or 'Yes, I was wrong', the barriers would disappear, and Elijah would stand forth, glittering in his glory and visible to us all.

QUINTIN HOGG

UNLESS the composition of the House of Lords is reformed, Quintin Hogg, eldest son of Lord Hailsham, and one of the ablest of the younger Conservative M.P.s, will one day suffer a kind of political death by exaltation.

Hogg is now a man of forty-one, of delicate features, but of a certain portliness, and with a premature development of that bowed carriage which might be termed statesman's stoop. His reputation began early. He distinguished himself at Eton and at Christ Church, where he got a double First, became a Fellow of All Souls at the age of twenty-four, practised at the Bar with a distinction which provoked comparisons with F. E. Smith, and won a brilliant by-election against a formidable opponent. When he entered the lists as candidate for Oxford City, shortly after Munich, public attention was fixed on him. His brief, to defend Mr Chamberlain, was one of critical importance to his party. Public anger against appeasement was rising, and the Master of Balliol, Mr Lindsay (now Lord Lindsay of Birker), decided to contest the seat. The electorate must have been somewhat bewildered by this contest between a professional philosopher of politics and a brilliant jurist. Mr Hogg was returned by a comfortable majority.

His parliamentary career, distinguished from the outset, was interrupted by the war. He served from 1939 to 1942 in the Rifle Brigade and was wounded. Then he returned to politics to found, with Peter Thorneycroft, the Tory Reform movement, which called up shades of Disraeli's Young England and stimulated much of the Coalition Government's social legislation. A few cracks of the Party Whip served only, as is usual in such cases, to focus attention on the Tory Reformers, and Mr Hogg traversed the well-worn track between political martyrdom and junior Ministerial office with unusual rapidity, becoming Under-Secretary of State for Air in 1945. In the long run it proved to be the party and not the Tory Reformers who capitulated. Meantime, Mr Hogg resumed his legal practice and has a growing reputation at the Bar.

It is impossible to understand all aspects of Quintin Hogg

without recalling the work of his grandfather of the same name, who founded the Regent Polytechnic and devoted his life to Christian philanthropy. From him Hogg inherits a passionate interest in individuals and an evangelical zeal in matters of social reform, which at first sight appear to accord ill with his legal approach to politics. Its basis is High Anglicanism, and Hogg is frequently to be seen in the congregation of St Margaret's, Westminster, parish church of the Commons and now the acknowledged centre of intellectual Anglicanism in London.

The Tory Reform movement was intended to remind the Conservative Party of its ancient tradition of social reform and of its part in the nineteenth century as the enemy of Liberal individualism. For forty years the Conservative Party has been looking for a programme at once reformist and conservative, a programme which does not consist merely in opposition to change or in the slavish imitation of its opponents. The Tory Reformers could not fill the bill, since their chief plank was increased social services, a programme common to nearly all parties since Bismarck invented it. But Tory Reform did provide the party with some much-needed oxygen and created the atmosphere in which an attempt to apply Conservative principles to current politics could be made.

Hogg wished to make the movement a kind of Right-Wing Fabian Society, a political laboratory and a power-house of ideas. After the General Election his increasing activities at the Bar, combined with his feelings that nothing should be done to suggest that the remnants of Toryism were divided, led to the gradual dissolution of the movement. Meantime, Peter Thorneycroft, one of its chief members, had embarked on his long courtship of the Liberal Party. Quintin Hogg was at first not particularly sympathetic, but when it seemed that the party might repudiate his friend he characteristically rallied to his side.

The distinguishing characteristic of his approach to contemporary politics is his belief that anti-intellectualism is the Conservative Party's chief vice. Labour's victory, he believes, was largely due to the conversion of the British intelligentsia to Socialist principles by twenty years of one-sided argumentation.

His campaign to make the Conservative Party the party of the most intelligent was recently inaugurated by the publication of his Penguin book, *The Case for Conservatism*. He applies the principles of Burkeian Conservatism to current politics with an analytical power and a forensic skill which few writers on either side can command. Everyone recognises that his book is a *tour de force*. It is too long for the average reader, but he does not mind that, as he is addressing himself deliberately to an exclusive audience. Ten years ago, when the assumption that an intelligent young man could not be a Conservative was fashionably at the universities, it would have attracted more attention than today when the swing of highbrow opinion is noticeably correcting itself. Strict purists will complain that it bears some traces of the pliable spirit of a Peel rather than the sterner mental habits of a Disraeli. But the book shows that its author is a worthy contender against the set views of the Conservative Central Office, which has long believed, in spite of the success of the Left Book Club, that the British have no interest whatsoever in political doctrine and care only for personalities and programmes.

As a parliamentarian Quintin Hogg suffers from what is known as 'fatal facility'. He scores points too easily, and loses his temper too often (at Oxford he knocked more than one of his contemporaries down). This defect is the reverse side of his deliberate courage, both moral and physical.

Hogg's ultimate destiny, if all goes well for him, seems most likely to be the Woolsack. Prime Ministers have to be on more intimate terms with the House and the nation than he is likely to find it easy to be. There is about his speech and writing a trace of the isolation of the intellectual, which deprives him of the popular touch of, for example, a Bevin or an Eden.

Meanwhile he is busy on his task of conversion. A skilled advocate with some of the missionary zeal of his grandfather, he may well play an important part in shaping the political life of this country in the next ten or twenty years. What is more doubtful is whether he will convert the Conservative Party to his views before the next election.

HAROLD WILSON

LONG before Harold Wilson entered Parliament, people in the Labour Movement had begun talking about him. He was a phenomenon, they said, a political infant prodigy. Even ten years ago, when he was scarcely twenty-two and was working eighteen hours a day with Lord Beveridge, men who had never seen him were prophesying a great career.

It is difficult to say on what this confidence was really based. True, Harold Wilson won a scholarship to Oxford and took a brilliant first; but, after all, other men had done that before him. He had published no books. He had made no particular mark in Oxford Labour circles, and indeed had little sympathy with the strong Communist influence there. He was not a natural orator. Yet the opinion persisted: Wilson was to be one of the future leaders of the Party.

In 1945 he was returned to Parliament, and his fellow members looked with some curiosity at this young man who had immediately been given a Ministerial post. They had expected to see a typical intellectual, dry and dusty from feeding on economic text books, and—the Labour Party being what it is—were prepared to be suspicious of him. They saw instead a young man of twenty-nine, chubbily friendly and human, with a taste for double-breasted waistcoats, and modest to the point of apparent timidity.

There were other surprises. As an intellectual Harold Wilson should have been a brilliant theoretician. The trade union members, shifting uneasily on their chairs in the smoke room, were relieved to find that he 'didn't know what Marx's theory of surplus value was and didn't want to know'.

Harold Wilson has very little in common with the pioneers of the Movement: he is neither a George Lansbury, believing that Socialism is the logical conclusion of Christianity, nor an H. M. Hyndman, prophesying that the class war would end in a glorious and flaming Armageddon. But it is equally difficult to identify him with any of the younger men who have made their mark in the Party during the last few years. He has none of Strachey's lucid grasp of Socialist theory. To say that he is a great administrator in the making is perhaps to give a misleading idea of him. Harold Wilson is more than this. He is that rare bird—an administrator who is never likely to forget his humanity or to think of men and women as tidy digits in a fascinating mathematical problem.

Through the Oxford voice there still runs, faint but unmistakable, the trace of a Yorkshire accent, broadening the vowels, thickening the words. Wilson, in fact, is a product of Yorkshire radicalism, which explains both his toughness as a negotiator as well as his freedom from prejudice. His father, a works chemist, was a strong Liberal, though he joined the Labour Party later on: just as the young Raleigh was treated with visions of the new world, so the young Harold was enthralled by stories of how the Liberals had massacred the Tories in 1906.

On the whole he must have had a delightfully normal and healthy childhood. He was always out of doors. When the *Yorkshire Evening Post* ran a competition called 'My Hero', the boy sent in an essay. It was on Baden-Powell. He spent long summer days watching Wilfred Rhodes bowl his beautiful, curving, deceptive slows. In the winter there was football and the adored Huddersfield Town.

Life would have been carefree enough but for rising unemployment and the menace, uncomfortably close, of poverty. Father and son held long serious discussions on the problem. 'What I don't understand', the boy said, 'is why Percy next door can't sell his woollen cloth to buy coal, and Bill in the local pit can't sell his coal to buy woollen cloth.' Even then he saw the problem in the terms of an equation which had to be solved, and it is curious to find how little his attitude has altered since then. Capitalism was an unworthy muddle rather than a corruption which called for a crusade on the part of the righteous. But Socialism was not an end in itself: it was necessary because it created the conditions in which a solution to the economic problem was possible.

The point comes out clearly in his book *New Deal for Coal*. Nationalisation was essential if only to restore the industry's morale. It would not, he wrote, 'solve the problem of industrial relations, but is an essential condition of a solution'. The same was true if the industry was to be run efficiently. 'Nationalisation will do no more than create conditions in which the skill and experience of mining engineers and miners will have full scope.' There speaks a Socialist without illusions and without obsessions.

Harold Wilson needed all his Yorkshire toughness when it came to the trade talks with Russia. The contrast between him and Mr Mikoyan, the head of the Soviet delegation, must have been fascinating to watch—the contrast between the young and vital Wilson and the older Mikoyan, haggard with years of negotiating agreements, with all the facts in his head and several aces up his sleeve, playing his hand with the sure experience of a master, and without any flicker of emotion on his fine and marble face.

People who took part in the talks say of Harold Wilson that he was always fresh despite the long and arduous hours. 'As soon as the door opened,' one of them says, 'it was like showing the ideal pond to a very vigorous duck.' It was just as well. On the last day the talks began at 7 p.m. and ended at six o'clock in the morning. Mikoyan and Wilson were still collected and fresh at the end of it, but several of their followers were stretched out on the chairs and sofas, and the agreement was initialled to a chorus of approving whistles and snores.

Perhaps few people realise that Harold Wilson was under a special temptation during those negotiations. He was a young man just beginning his career: what a triumph to bring back an agreement after so many had failed. In the first round during the summer the temptation must have been almost insupportable. Everything had been settled—the amounts and the prices —and only the means of payment remained. The Russian proposals would have meant a loss of dollars from our very slender resources, and the question for Wilson was whether he should cable for fresh instructions, urging the Cabinet to accept the Soviet terms. He resolutely refused to do so. Courage and strength of character must be added to his proved gift of a quick and brilliant mind.

ANEURIN BEVAN

FOR several of the war years Aneurin Bevan—'that architect of disloyalty', as Mr Churchill once called him in a heated moment—was known as the most turbulent M.P. on the Opposition benches, and at one time his own Party came near to expelling him for voting against the Government on a major issue. His weekly paper *Tribune*, whose editorship-in-chief he had inherited from Sir Stafford Cripps, also criticised the conduct of the war, and British foreign policy, with a freedom that sometimes bordered on irresponsibility. These activities have tended to stamp him in the public mind as the naughty boy of the Labour Party and to obscure the solid achievements that actually lie behind him.

Aneurin Bevan was born in 1897, the son of a coalminer. He himself left school at thirteen and went to work in the pit. In spite of his powerful physique he was a shy, bookish boy, left-handed, and troubled by a severe stammer, which still has a slight tendency to return in moments when he is overtired. In such spare time as he could get he read voraciously, making a speciality of books on philosophy. He had the chance to educate himself, he says, quite largely because the Tredegar public library happened to be an exceptionally good one and the librarian took a personal interest in him. As for his stammer and his nervousness, he got rid of them by deliberately involving himself in street-corner meetings and other situations where he knew he would be compelled to speak extempore.

Some years later he was able to leave the pit and study at the Central Labour College. He was only nineteen when he was chairman of the largest Miners' lodge in South Wales, and was still a very young man when he became a member of the local Urban District Council. He was a miners' disputes agent in 1926, and has held the Ebbw Vale seat since 1929. With this background his natural affinity might seem to be with the trade union end of the Labour Party, but in fact he has until lately been looked on with some suspicion by the chiefs of the T.U.C.

His following, outside his own constituency, has been chiefly among the 'intellectuals' of the Party branches and the growing body of middle-class people whose sympathies have turned leftward during the past five or ten years. He was the close associate of Sir Stafford Cripps until Cripps joined the Churchill Government, and he has many foreign refugee Socialists among his friends and advisers. He is more of an extremist and more of an internationalist than the average Labour M.P., and it is the combination of this with his working-class origin that makes him an interesting and unusual figure.

On any issue of domestic policy—on housing, social security, education, public health—Bevan thinks and feels as a working man. He knows how the scales are weighted against anyone with less than £5 a week, and during the war he has defended the right of the workers to strike, even at moments when strikes did or could seriously hamper the war effort. But he is remarkably free—some of his adversaries would say dangerously free—from any feeling of personal grievance against society. He shows no sign of ordinary class consciousness. He seems equally at home in all kinds of company. It is difficult to imagine anyone less impressed by social status or less inclined to put on airs with subordinates. Everyone who has more than a nodding acquaintance with him calls him by his nickname of 'Nye'. He has the temperament that used to be called 'mercurial'—a temperament capable of sudden low spirits but not of settled pessimism. His boisterous manner sometimes gives casual observers the impression that he is not serious, and his warmest admirers do not claim that punctuality is his strong point. But in fact he has a huge capacity for work and manages to put in a great deal of time at his rather inaccessible constituency.

Some of Bevan's qualities may be traceable to his Welsh blood. Though only tepidly interested in Welsh Nationalism, he has not lost touch with his origins and retains traces of his Welsh accent. His infrequent holidays are always devoted to climbing in his native hills. He is a typical Celt not only in his quickness of speech and abrupt alternations of mood but in his respect for the intellect. He does not have the suspicion of 'cleverness' and anaesthesia to the arts which are generally regarded as the mark of a practical man. Those who have worked with him in a journalistic capacity have remarked with pleasure and astonishment that here at last is a politician who knows that literature exists and will even hold up work for five minutes to discuss a point of style.

Bevan's campaign against Churchill, in Parliament and in the press, was very bitter, and sometimes undignified. There were moments when Bevan seemed to be actuated by personal dislike, and Churchill, too, was more easily 'drawn' by Bevan than by any other opponent. Some observers have remarked that the two men are natural antagonists 'because they are so alike'. In fact, there are points of resemblance. Both men are naturally genial but capable of sudden anger and rough speech, both of them have been held back in their careers by the 'cleverness' which did not commend itself to more stolid colleagues. Whether Bevan is fully Churchill's equal in obstinacy remains to be seen.

The post he now holds, a post in which he is responsible not only for public health but for rehousing, is a thankless and difficult one. In the matter of houses the public expects miracles and is certain to be disappointed at not getting them. Bevan is well aware of this. He sought out his present job because he feels strongly about slum clearance, about the effects of the housing shortage on the birthrate, and about the need to put the practice of medicine on a non-commercial basis. Those who know him believe that he can make decisions boldly, will get results, and will soon be more than just a fiery debater in the public eye.

EDITH SUMMERSKILL

LIFE is not as heady as in the roaring, crusading 'thirties. Everything wore a simple look then. Rearmament was a racket, the Peace Ballot a nice idea, Geneva a sure poultice (if only silly people would use it!) against all the boils of Europe.

Dr Edith rode on the crest of this congenial wave. Did Power for the Left seem faintly improbable? No matter: the radiance of winged victory already shone about her person, a foreglow, as it were, of July, 1945. Dr Edith's flashing smile, her tall comeliness, the cold whipcrack of her platform voice gave faith to the faltering and certitude to the sturdy.

When she got in at West Fulham (1938) the crowd roped her car and hauled their heroine through festal streets. The Left was still young and eager, its brow unseamed by the cares of office. To the sound of a Sunday afternoon bugle, throngs at four platforms in Hyde Park passed a withering anti-Franco resolution. Dr Edith was there, orating with Clement Attlee from the same coal cart.

Nobody with a sense of duty would relinquish Treasury Bench for coal cart; but is not coal cart in some aspects better fun? One doubts whether such questions ever occur to Dr Edith. She is not in the habit of looking sentimentally over her shoulder. She has always lived, and usually rev lled, in the present, whether learning to be a doctor (King's College and Charing Cross Hospital), fighting a county council seat, looking at health services in Spain, Russia, and Italy, or speaking for her Ministry at Geneva.

As Parliamentary Secretary to the Minister of Food she has for nearly three years been immersed, absorbed, overworked, and entirely happy. Turn and turn about with Mr Strachey, she goes into action at Question Time in the Commons, trimly tailored and rather a Tartar. Severity is mitigated by a rope of pearls. The Opposition may bait or bellow about soap powder or bread rationing. Her smile is always secure. Did somebody once ask for a change from the odious monotony of 'mousetrap' cheese? The Doctor would not 'pander' to such a sybarite. Her observations on food have sometimes suggested that she regards the art of eating merely as the exercise of Nutritional Intake. Question after question, supplementary after supplementary, is disposed of in level, metallic tones. Questioners are sometimes put in their place with a quip as laconic as a snap fastener.

For the voice which orated from the coal cart is now the organ of a Department, a vast, vague, frightening thing. At Montagu House Dr Edith sits behind a desk in a second floor bay window flooded in season with sunshine, from which, when she has a second to spare, she can see barges sailing past the County Hall. The windows are attractively curtained. Dr Edith insisted that it should be so. And the Ministry of Works complied. No other room in Montagu House has curtains of any sort.

In neighbouring rooms six women secretaries toil laboriously in Dr Edith's wake from Monday morning till Friday night. They keep track of many things. Here is a deputation of milkmen from the West Country. Here is a parcel of publicans from the Midlands. Here are councillors from a London borough. They want to know if Dr Edith cannot do something about wicked ice-cream sellers who pump air into their ice-cream so that there will seem to be more of it. Then there is the constant thundershower of Members' complaints and queries. All of which implies endless talks with officials, muggings-up of fact and figure, minute briefings, and a quite exceptional talent for hacking one's way through copses of detail.

Office has in no way slaked Dr Edith's rampant feminism. She is still earnest about the reform project popularly known as Wages for Wives. The male who voices a timorous doubt whether Acts of Parliament are the best way of dealing with connubial economics will more likely than not be silenced with: 'But you are a man. You don't understand. Men do not understand these things. They are too emotional.' Which, of course, is the death of dialectics.

Along with the metallic detachment of her Question Time performances goes a doctrinaire impulsiveness which sometimes involves her in chilly utterances. It would be hard to

EDITH SUMMERSKILL

imagine any slogan more dismal than 'Socialism must begin in the home'. Or any generalisation more steely than: 'A woman having a baby is supplying one of the most important pieces of machinery—if I may call a baby a piece of machinery—of the State.'

Neither Dr Summerskill nor anybody else may rationally call a baby anything of the sort. The consoling thing is that this unhappy image comes from a conspicuously happy wife, mother and home-maker, who has always, in human terms, put first things first. Nobody is more fervent about careers for women. Yet she has been heard to say that, if her husband were not of the enlightened kind, if he were grumpy because she is rarely at home in the evenings, she would give up politics and for harmony's sake become a routine housewife.

Home atmosphere and influence are, in her view, paramount. That is why the two children of Dr and Mrs E. Jeffrey Samuel (to quote Dr Edith's married style) went to day-schools, whence they could come home each evening for parental affection and comradeship, rather than to boarding schools, 'which are excellent for children with unhappy homes, but not for the rest'.

Love in the Home is, indeed, one of Dr Edith's salient themes, an important mollifying factor in her personal brand of Socialism. The flat in Kensington (plenty of books, snug fireside, here and there an antique) is innocent of regimentation. The four Samuels have a joint hobby: family reunion.

In all these matters Dr Edith is richly typical of the middle wing of English Socialism which, doctrine or no doctrine, is as devotedly domestic as the Victorians ever were. On Sundays, when departmental homework is not knee-deep at the fireside, Dr Edith takes the Sealyham for a walk in Kensington Gardens. Prince Albert, one is sure, looks down upon her from his memorial dais with a disapproval not entirely unmixed.

ISAAC FOOT

THERE are two things to remember about Isaac Foot, the President of the Liberal Party Organisation. He is a Nonconformist and he comes from the West Country. Politics for him will never be a matter of shifts and expedients, still less of blue books and statistics. They are the constant application of first principles, proclaimed with a Devonshire accent.

He was born in 1880 in a family as irreproachably proletarian as that of any Labour leader. He was one of seven children who were reared on a domestic budget of a pound a week and he began life as a Civil Service clerk at a weekly wage of 14s., rising at the end of the first year to 15s. He represents, however, a different tradition from most of our present rulers. The community in which he was brought up owed its loyalty to the chapel and not to the trade union. The struggle was not against the employer but against the landlord and the parson. The result is an attitude of mind which, although antipathetic to the Tory Party and all its works, is none the less far removed from Socialism.

The emphasis is upon the individual and not upon the team. Your militant Nonconformist Liberal, no less than your doctrinaire Marxist, is on the side of the underdog, but it is almost always a particular, identifiable underdog and not underdogs as a class—a soul to be saved, not an average to be adjusted. Indeed it is probably true to say that men of this stamp oppose Toryism and Socialism for precisely the same reasons. Their instinct is always to be against authority and they dislike the rôle of the commissar no less than the rule of the patrician and the priest.

Isaac Foot has fought twelve Parliamentary elections and represented the Bodmin Division of Cornwall in five Parliaments. From August, 1931, until September, 1932, he was Secretary for Mines. His temperament and training made it comparatively easy for him to understand the outlook of the miners, and within a few months he had established surprisingly cordial relations both with the miners' leaders and with their representatives in the House of Commons. When the Liberal

Ministers resigned in protest against the Ottawa agreements, it was a great sacrifice to give up a post for which he was so peculiarly suited and to leave work in which he was completely absorbed. But no one who knows Isaac Foot would suspect him of a moment's hesitation. He had nothing but contempt for the trimmers whose free trade convictions had vanished almost overnight. If there is one thing which he finds it hard to forgive or understand it is political apostasy. So he resigned and went with Sir Herbert Samuel and Sir Archibald Sinclair, first to the benches below the gangway and later into outright opposition.

Apart from the mines and the tariff issue his main interest during the 'thirties was India. He was a member of the Round Table Conference in 1930 and of the Joint Select Committee in 1933, and in 1935 he took an exceedingly prominent part in the debates on the Government of India Bill. One of his most treasured possessions is a personal letter from Dr Ambedkar, the leader of the Depressed Classes, thanking him for his constant efforts on their behalf. No tribute to his services has ever given him greater satisfaction. But it was dearly earned for it was largely his preoccupation with Indian affairs which led to the loss of his Cornish seat at the General Election of 1935. His critics were not slow to suggest that thinking imperially was no fit occupation for a West Country Member of Parliament, who should be expected to concentrate his entire attention upon broccoli and pilchards.

Isaac's enthusiasms are book-collecting, history, literature, and everything to do with Cromwell. At his Cornish home he has accumulated over forty thousand books, and the never-ending flood overflows into any other building of which he is the permanent or temporary occupier. During the war he served on the Security Executive, and the astonished representatives of M.I.5 or other kindred organisations found themselves discussing the problems of national security amidst steadily encroaching piles of first editions. But his library, like that of the Emperor Gordianus, is for use rather than ostentation. At various times he has taught himself French, German, and classical Greek, and the range of his studies is immense. As a result he possesses an astonishing repertory of quotations, and a political opponent is liable to find himself suddenly transfixed by a shaft borrowed from Shakespeare, Cromwell, Junius, Burke or Macaulay. There was, for example, the unfortunate Minister in the first labour Government who, somewhat haughtily, endeavoured to dispose of a parliamentary question by a reference to 'the law's delays'. 'And', said Mr Foot completing the quotation, 'the insolence of office.'

Most marked of all is his historical sense. He is certainly one of those for whom the roots of the present lie deep in the past. When he was Lord Mayor of Plymouth, he set himself to make the city conscious of its own famous history. By November, 1946, when Isaac Foot completed his year of office, there was scarcely a schoolchild in the city who could not have given a succinct account of the three-years' siege, the defeat of the Armada and the voyage of the Golden Hind.

As President of the Liberal Party Organisation he is not a mere figurehead. He has thrown all his powers into the campaign to make the Liberal Party once more an effective force in British politics. For Liberalism, as Isaac Foot understands it, is not a pallid compromise between rival extremes. Still less is it the legacy of Victorian economists. For him it is the cause for which Hampden died in the field and Sydney on the scaffold.

LORD WINTERTON

WHATEVER else anybody may think of him—and there are certainly many views—nobody can doubt that Edward Turnour, 6th Earl Winterton, is, to his very depths, a 'House of Commons man'. He has been there, man and boy, for more than forty years, and was first elected so young that he became Father of the House of Commons at the precocious age of sixty-two.

There was something singularly appropriate in his election as Chairman of the Select Committee which planned the new House of Commons after the Luftwaffe had destroyed the old on 10 May 1941. For Winterton's whole life is centred in the Commons. There can be few Members—if any—who attend more regularly, or for longer hours, than he.

Though he still holds to the extreme Right on some subjects, he has ranked himself with the 'young Tories' by joining—in the rather detached and independent way he 'joins' things—the progressively minded Tory Reform Committee. It is typical of a man whose spirit is too keen and eager ever to grow old, and who is too much of an individualist to fit any political pigeon-hole.

His readiness and ability to intervene in a dying debate with some matter of 'the greatest constitutional importance'—he is an adept at finding such issues—has at times done little to endear him to his fellow Members or to the Commons staff. But all admire the dogged persistence with which he hangs on to a point he conceives to be of importance.

Lord Winterton, it has been said, looks more like the *Vanity Fair* cartoon of himself than any other cartoonist's victim ever did. Tall and extremely slender, he favours tight jackets and too-short 'drainpipe' trousers, which emphasise his physical build and make him a figure at whom even the most casual passer-by must glance more than once.

When, out of doors, he adds a bowler hat of ample proportions, which he squashes down over his ears, the ensemble is truly striking. In the hunting field, where he is an ardent and gallant performer, he wears the pink and looks no less remarkable. He is very fond of clubs and company.

OBSERVER PROFILES

Winterton's is not the gentlest temper in the House, and he is apt to be intolerant and autocratic, to launch into a peppery tirade, on the smallest provocation, or on none. But his mental outlook is essentially a just one; he is always ready to flare up at what seems to him an injustice, whether to an unpopular fellow-Member or to some quite obscure fellow-citizen.

There is no M.P. who more vociferously maintains the rights of the House of Commons, none who more insistently upholds his own rights and privileges. To see Lord Winterton rapping imperiously on the Westminster kerbstones with a demand that the police stop the traffic to facilitate his passage to the House of Commons is an impressive sight.

Yet he knows he is right—he is always right in his own estimation—for does not the House, at the opening of each new Session, solemnly order the Commissioner of Police for the Metropolis to 'take care that the passages through the streets leading to this House be kept free and open'? The fact that that resolution originated, probably, in some attempt to blockade Parliament, back in the Middle Ages, is nothing to him. To his literal mind, a clear street is a clear street, and he will rap till Parliament's orders are carried out.

He does not suffer fools gladly, or, indeed, at all. And he has an extensive list of people he classes as fools. To him, a feud is something to be pursued, in season and out, with Hibernian persistence—his is an Irish Earldom—until the other man cries 'Quits!' And then it is all promptly forgotten, the hatchet is buried, and peace reigns until further cause for feud arises.

The seemingly endless wordy battle he had with Mr Tom Shaw, a leading Socialist Member, the better part of twenty years ago, is still remembered. Winterton was Under-Secretary at the India Office at the time, and he engaged in round after round, day after day, until the House was weary and bored, and his bony hands seemed about to shatter from his unceasing battering of the dispatch box. No doubt 'twas a famous victory, but, as with Peterkin, the House never quite knew what it was all about.

Full marks for discretion he would never earn, but for courage the highest marks would be inadequate. The House of Commons, angry, can be a snarling, intimidating creature to most—but not to 'Eddie' Winterton. Strong men have quailed before the frown of Mr Churchill as Prime Minister, given him best without a struggle—but not Winterton.

His mannerisms are famous. Angry or triumphant, he will rub his lean hands together at a speed that threatens at any moment to produce first smoke, then flame. In debate he will wind his legs around each other in frightening contortion, sway his long body back and forth in an equilibration Richard Hearne might envy.

But if the House does sometimes laugh at him he is no figure of fun. No Minister dare ignore his points or can afford to spurn his praise. None but the most callow back-bencher treads on his political corns. For he will uphold fully the dignity and importance of what he, with modest pride, calls 'that paternal position in which I find myself'.

Perhaps just because he *is* so good a House of Commons man Winterton shines more in opposition than in office. Truth to tell, he was not a resounding success in office—he held many posts—industrious and painstaking as he was. But give him someone else's Bill and he will worry the last inequality, the ultimate inconsistency out of it. Give him a grievance, and he will 'raise this matter of great constitutional importance' until something is done about it.

At sixty-two there is still a good deal of the Old Etonian, New College, Oxford, undergraduate who (at the age of twenty-one) strolled nonchalantly into the House of Commons in November, 1904. He has stayed ever since, with a characteristically gallant and dashing military interlude in the 1914–18 war, when he served in Gallipoli and Palestine, was twice mentioned in despatches, took part in the famous desert campaign which led to the fall of Damascus, and won the firm friendship of T. E. Lawrence and the Emir Feisal.

In the course of years the Baby of the House has become its Father—but without growing up too much.

PERIOD PIECES

SENATOR TRUMAN
1944

SENATOR HARRY TRUMAN says about his ancestry, 'We are a little of everything. If you shook the family tree, anything might fall out—Scotch, Irish, and Dutch stock would be there for certain.'

No one was more surprised than Truman when he was adopted Democratic candidate for the Vice-Presidency. He went to the Chicago Democratic Convention primed to promote James Byrnes for the post. When support began to develop for himself, he had repeatedly to be reassured that he was really Mr Roosevelt's choice.

The choice fell on Truman because his labour record was acceptable to the C.I.O., because his past association with the Kansas City political machine made him acceptable to the city bosses, because in running the Truman Committee of the Senate to investigate the national defence effort he had become a national symbol of criticism of Government waste, and because his State, Missouri, is a border State whose support must be wooed in a close election campaign.

Truman is modest, kindly, simple, straightforward, and honest. Many are surprised at the word honest, because he got into politics through the notorious Boss Pendergast political machine which ran Kansas City and Missouri through the 'twenties and 'thirties: ran it wide open for vice and graft—until Boss Pendergast was caught out by the Federal District Attorney, Maurice Milligan, for taking bribes from fire insurance companies, and went to jail for income tax evasion.

Harry Truman was born in Missouri in 1884 and moved to a farm at Independence when he was four. He was a serious boy labelled 'Sissy' by the town toughs. He could not go to West Point, the American Sandhurst, because his eyes were weak.

SENATOR TRUMAN

He became a timekeeper for the Santa Fé railroad, a clerk in a bank, rose to book-keeper, then went back to his father's farm for ten years to plough the straightest row of corn his mother ever saw. A captain of artillery in France in the last war, he went back home to open a haberdashery store in Kansas City, which left him fourteen years later still paying off its £3,000 debts. He married his childhood playmate and has one daughter, Mary Margaret.

Backed by the American Legion veterans of the last war in 1921, he got the support of Boss Pendergast for an elective job as a county judge in Jackson County, Missouri. He had had two years at Kansas City School of Law. He became a presiding judge, and stayed there until 1934. That put him over the county road supervisors, and it is his pride that under his control £5,000,000 were spent in improving roads and public buildings. He had a rigorously honest record in spending the money. But he got restless and wanted to become a tax collector, a more remunerative office. Tom Pendergast said he had promised that job to someone else and, as the famous story now goes, said, 'The best I can do right now, Harry, is a United States Senatorship'. Truman won the election in 1935 for a six-year term in Washington, during which he said little and voted consistently for the New Deal programme. In 1940 he ran for re-election and won, because the same Maurice Milligan, who put Pendergast in prison, split the opposition vote with a third candidate, and Truman slipped through.

He became interested in stopping wasteful Government expenditure, and got the Senate to appoint a committee to investigate the national defence effort, with some of the ablest Senators on it, under his chairmanship. It developed a record for honesty and thoroughness which made him nationally famous and made his committee the nearest United States equivalent to a Parliamentary Select Committee on Public Accounts. This was largely the work of a lawyer he secured to run the committee, procedure, and staff—Hugh Fulton, a former Wall Street lawyer from the Department of Justice. As a Democrat he did not want to smear his party's administration and wanted to make it more efficient. That led to his name coming to the fore at Chicago when the managers were working to get rid of Henry Wallace. In the campaign he worked hard, travelled far, made many speeches, and left the impression of being just what he is—an average American from Missouri, a State characterised by the familiar American saying, when a new idea or proposition comes up: 'I'm from Missouri. I've got to be shown'.

The Republican opposition did its best to make political hay of his past association with the corrupt Pendergast machine, but did not make any headway in loading the machine's dishonesties on him personally. The Hearst Press labelled him a member of the infamous reactionary 'Ku Klux Klan', but Truman nailed the story as a lie.

He raised no famous issues in his election speeches except to call on Mr Dewey to repudiate the Isolationist Senators of the Republican Party, who would be in powerful positions in Congress if the Republicans should win. Mr Dewey ignored the challenge. Truman put his foot in it hard with his statement that Senator Walsh, Democrat, of Massachusetts, and chairman of the Senate Naval Affairs Committee, was just as much an Isolationist as the Republicans except, said Truman, that 'we have a chance to reform him'. Walsh was insulted, but his support is believed important in Massachusetts, and President Roosevelt had to go out of his way to appease Walsh.

Probably Truman didn't add one vote to Mr Roosevelt's strength in the election, but he did not lose him any. His border State, Missouri, did finally support Mr Roosevelt, but for a time even this was doubtful.

His job, as Vice-President, will be to preside over the Senate, and he aims to try to rebuild some co-operation between Congress and the Executive. Most Vice-Presidents, unlike Henry Wallace, confine themselves to this Senate job. And Truman will probably do the same. Because that is a critical issue with the Democratic Party if, in the next four years, it is to prepare for the absence of Mr Roosevelt as a candidate in the 1948 elections.

SENATOR TRUMAN

The Republicans made much of the fact that if the President dies, the Vice-President becomes President for the rest of the term. Six Presidents have died in office. Harry Truman, quiet and grey, is not an inspiring man with any deep-rooted infectious idealism. So he would not make a great President. But, by the same token, he would not be the worst President. He could probably be labelled a good Vice-President, but a mediocre candidate for President.

GENERAL DE GAULLE
Leader of 'Fighting France'—1943

CHARLES ANDRÉ JOSEPH MARIE DE GAULLE was born in the provincial town of Lille fifty-three years ago. His father was a soldier of strong religious beliefs. When a law was passed in the early years of this century making it illegal for Jesuit priests to teach in French colleges, de Gaulle *père* became the first lay 'prefect of studies' at the Jesuit College in the Rue de Vaugirard in Paris.

Charles was educated at the Jesuit school in the Rue des Postes which prepared boys intending to become army officers. At the famous military college of St Cyr he belonged to the small category of Jesuit-trained cadets known as *Postards*.

On leaving St Cyr in 1912, his request to join the 33rd Infantry Regiment was granted. He had selected this regiment, his biographer, Philippe Barrès, informs us, out of admiration for its colonel, Philippe Pétain. The future was to bring these two men close together before their ways diverged.

De Gaulle fought most gallantly as a junior officer in the 1914–18 war. He was wounded three times; on the last occasion he was taken prisoner. He made several attempts to escape from the prison camp, after which he was transferred to a special fortress with other Allied officers who had done likewise.

Here he made the acquaintance of a young and ambitious Russian officer—Tukhachevsky. Later, in 1921, they were on opposite sides when de Gaulle served under Weygand against the Bolsheviks in Poland.

After this, the great Pétain began to take a friendly interest in him. It was Pétain who had him appointed an instructor at the École de Guerre, and attended in person his first lecture. Later, Pétain took him on to his own staff as his A.D.C., in which post he remained as long as Pétain was Commander-in-Chief of the Army. Thus he passed his thirties amongst those French officers who are of the extreme Right, staunch Catholics and Nationalists and, by habit, somewhat unfriendly to this country and its empire which is everywhere neighbour to their own.

GENERAL DE GAULLE

But Charles de Gaulle was never quite the typical French officer. As well as possessing a distinctive physique—tall, slackly built, with features that are somewhat morose when at rest but transformed with energy when speaking to more than one person—his mind and temper are equally unusual. He has a mobile and inventive intellect, with a tendency towards the dramatic and the picturesque: a strong will and a dominating temperament.

While his private manner is aloof, even cold, and speech deliberate, there is an emotional power in him which can be communicated to the many. With little humour, much love of discipline, a passion for all to do with war, and a fervent nationalist ardour, he has always been a man with few personal friends but with a certain following.

The year of Hitler's impressive rise to power, 1933, saw de Gaulle once more close to Pétain. The Marshal was President of the Conseil Supérieur de la Guerre; de Gaulle had become its Secretary-General. While all Europe was still discussing the Hitler *coup*, de Gaulle published in 1934 his very remarkable book, *The Army of the Future*, now so much spoken of as the military doctrine which might have saved France in 1940. It advocated the creation of a mechanised *corps d'élites* of only 100,000 men with special privileges. Few have troubled to study this book, even though it has been publicly suggested that it envisaged the creation of a small professional army for internal political purposes. Soon after this publication de Gaulle gave a series of lectures in the Sorbonne at the invitation of the students of the fascist *Action Française* party.

There is no question that de Gaulle understood modern war as Guderian and the German General Staff understood it, and that his military perspicacity is great. His advocacy of mechanised striking forces was hampered in France by his linking it with the demand for a professional standing army. This was in contradiction to France's Republican tradition of a large conscript army. He realised that only a strong man using unconventional means could bring about such a drastic change. Though on political matters his language is sometimes ambiguous, on this point he was precise. He wrote in a context worthy of close study (p. 157): 'A leader will have to appear.' In parts its language and phraseology show definite signs that its author had been influenced by Hitler's success in Germany, which resulted in the German Army receiving first priority in the State. The philosophy of its author is clearly summarised in its concluding sentence: 'For the sword is the axis of the world, and greatness cannot be shared.'

De Gaulle later repeated his 'modern' politico-military theses in a second book, *La France et son Armée*, affectionately dedicated to Pétain, who had become godfather to the son de Gaulle named Philippe in honour of the Marshal.

Shortly before the present war Colonel de Gaulle found in Reynaud a tentative listener to his military doctrines, which had meanwhile been considerably adapted to the needs of the coming war. Reynaud put them before the Chamber of Deputies, which rejected them.

When Reynaud, the pocket 'strong man', replaced Daladier as Premier in March, 1940, he hastily formed a new Government in his attempt to check the full flood of German power. He remembered the energetic Colonel de Gaulle, who had again put forward an able memorandum in January, 1940, and who was doing very well in command of the 4th Armoured Division, being promoted to General. At this time his main interest was still in military matters and command in the field.

More power for de Gaulle was generally welcomed by the Republican press. Other more surprising people revealed themselves as his friends. The prominent Fascist-Royalist Maurras wrote favourably of de Gaulle and his military theories in his paper, *Action Française*, on 3 June 1940, describing himself as a 'possibly compromising friend' of de Gaulle. On 7 June Reynaud appointed him Under-Secretary of State for War. On 9 June Léon Daudet, not known for political impartiality in his journalism, greeted the appointment of de Gaulle warmly in *Action Française*. So did the third leader of the Royalist party, Maurice Pujo, on the same day and in the same paper.

Events were now moving far too rapidly for de Gaulle's

military influence to make itself felt. He flew backwards and forwards from Paris to London, but nothing could stop the Panzer divisions that were later to drive the far larger Russian armies back for a greater distance than the breadth of France. France fell, defeated and dazed beyond all reckoning.

When at the time of the armistice de Gaulle decided to stay on in London, he was taken to see Mr Churchill by the ardently francophile Conservative M.P., Major-General E. L. Spears. De Gaulle was still almost unknown in London. He had a good military reputation, but nothing was known of his political views, other than that he believed passionately in France. The lack of any leading French civilian and the real desire of Mr Churchill to encourage the French people to resist brought the full power of the Foreign Office, the Treasury and of the B.B.C. behind the suggestion that he should head a Legion of Volunteers. It was intended to be a purely military venture, as the published text of the original Churchill-de Gaulle agreement testifies. The hope was gradually to recruit a million men. And though nothing like this number was ever achieved, it was a gallant idea that impressed the world.

But the civil organisation, which de Gaulle obtained permission from the British Government to create 'for the administration of his forces', opened up the possibility of future political power in France. 'Gaullism' was born. The main means of creating and developing this were a partial monopoly of broadcasting and a Secret Service organisation largely controlling, amongst other things, travel to and from France. The formidable and various uses which the solemn officer who wrote politico-military books has made of this exceptional opportunity is current unwritten history.

Since the summer of 1942 he has repeatedly pledged himself to respect the French Republican Constitution, and on 14 July of this year he declared himself in a Bastille Day speech to be the friend of Freedom and the Fourth Republic.

STANISLAW MIKOLAJCZYK
Prime Minister of the Polish Government in London—1944

STANISLAW MIKOLAJCZYK, the present Polish Prime Minister, was born in 1901, the son of a Polish farm labourer. Poznania, where the Mikolajczyk family lived, was under German rule. There the whole weight of the German *Drang nach Osten* hit the Poles. The colonisation carried on by Bismarck, and the mass expulsion of Polish peasants from their homes were still fresh memories in the years of Mikolajczyk's childhood. By that time, Poles were no longer expelled by force, but they were not allowed by law to build or own houses on their land. Polish peasants were denied not the land under their feet but a roof over their heads. The difference was not great. In the bitter struggle in Poznania the Polish peasant used all his innate stubbornness and cunning. The most famous episode was that of the 'Drzymala cart'. A peasant called Drzymala made his family's house in a hut on wheels; for months on end he contested his right to live in it. The clever Prussian lawyer who had made the anti-Polish law had made no provision against such a case. Poles had been forbidden to build houses, but not to live in carts. This was the environment and the atmosphere in which the Polish Prime Minister grew up.

Stanislaw's father was even less fortunate than the famous Drzymala. He possessed no land on which to put a 'house on wheels'. So he emigrated to Westphalia and worked there for ten years. The son was sent to a German school. During the ten years of his stay in Westphalia, the old Mikolajczyk saved every penny he could. In 1910 he returned to Poznania and bought a farm of fifty acres. These are the other features in the character of the Polish peasant, at least in Western Poland: patience and frugality.

True, there was not enough money to send Stanislaw to school. At the age of sixteen the boy was working in a sugar-beet refinery. But he acquired some knowledge in the hardness of life. And after the death of his father—about 1920—he inherited the farm and developed an active interest in the economic and political problems of farming. In his province he founded the Farm Youth Union. Soon he established his reputation as a moderate and successful peasants' leader. His election to the post of chairman of the Farming Associations in Poznania in the early thirties shocked the landed gentry. But after meeting this man, the landlords of Poznania satisfied themselves that Mikolajczyk's leanings were conservative rather than radical. So they accepted his leadership.

He started his Parliamentary career in 1930, when he was elected to the Sejm and became Secretary of the Parliamentary Group of the Peasant Party. 1930 was the year of a grave political crisis in Poland. The Peasant Party formed a bloc with the Socialists. Their aim was to re-establish parliamentary rule which had been destroyed by Pilsudski's *coup d'état* in 1926. The electoral campaign showed that the bloc of the Centre and the Left had a good chance of winning a majority. Pilsudski was scared: and he staged another *coup*. Shortly before the elections the principal members of the bloc were arrested and tortured in the fortress of Brest Litovsk. The opposition lost its leaders; the electorate was terrorised; the results of the vote were crudely falsified; and the military dictatorship was again firm in the saddle. Here was one aspect of Polish politics. During the great peasant strike which swept Poland in 1937, Mikolajczyk assumed for a time the formal chairmanship of the party, since the leader of the party, Witos, went into exile. After the strike he resigned because the permanent title was still reserved for the 'great exile'. The momentum of the peasants' demonstrations and strikes grew by leaps and bounds. When, in 1938, Rydz Smigly—Pilsudski's successor—suddenly made his appearance at one of those demonstrations, more than a hundred thousand peasants marched past him with the cry: 'We demand the return of Witos'. To bring together such masses of peasants from hundreds of miserable villages was quite an unusual feat of organisation and drive; and Mikolajczyk played a notable part.

In September, 1939, he fought as a private in the Polish campaign. Through Hungary he escaped to France; and became vice-chairman of the Polish National Council, formed by

General Sikorski. Its chairman was Paderewski, the great musician. It was perhaps difficult to find a sharper contrast than that between the chairman and the vice-chairman of the Council. The grey-haired, subtle, and noble head of the artist seemed to embody the spirit of Polish art. The bald, reddish, and somewhat crude but firm and stubborn face of Mikolajczyk seemed, by its very presence, to speak for the rustic body of Poland. In 1941, after General Sosnkowski resigned from the Polish Government in protest against the agreement with Russia, signed by General Sikorski, Mikolajczyk became Deputy Prime Minister; and after General Sikorski's death he became Prime Minister and leader of the coalition of four parties which participate in his Government. He is the first civilian premier Poland has had for many years—a fact which marks some progress in a country where official politics were, and partly still are, deeply sunk in the worship of military big-wigs. His appointment to the post of Prime Minister was to the supporters of the Pilsudski régime—and they are much more numerous in exile than in Poland itself—a shock similar to that which the landlords of Poznania experienced when Mikolajczyk was elected chairman of the Farming Associations in Poznania. Since then he has done much, probably too much, to appease the irreconcilable opposition.

But this is an affair of Polish domestic policy; and M. Mikolajczyk is now in the centre of a storm in Poland's foreign affairs. What he now defends may perhaps be not Poland's prewar frontiers but its independence. If the evolution of the Polish-Soviet conflict proves that this is the case, then M. Mikolajczyk may claim to speak for an overwhelming majority of his countrymen. Whatever the divisions in Poland's domestic policy—and they are deep and serious enough—there can be no doubt that M. Mikolajczyk does represent the stubborn will of his country to preserve its national individuality.

TRYGVE LIE
Acting Foreign Minister of Norway—1945

A CERTAIN lady, when asked by her dinner companion if she believed in euthanasia, replied that she believed in youth anywhere. This remark would have been enthusiastically echoed by Mr Trygve Lie, Norway's Minister of Foreign Affairs. From the age of four, bribed by liberal portions of ice-cream, his little daughters attended meetings addressed by their father.

Trygve Lie's own political career can be said to have started at the age of ten. Borrowing a horse and cart during election time he zealously toured the outlying districts of Aker, offering free lifts to the aged and infirm. When the cart was overflowing with gratified passengers, Lie cautiously canvassed their political opinons, expanding with such eloquence on his own, that either from exhaustion, as the drive grew longer and longer, or possibly conviction, they would announce their decision to vote for Labour, and were speeded into the Aker polling booths. The burning enthusiasm of that small boy still inspires the tough and practical thinker Lie is today.

Born in 1896 he joined the Labour Party when he was fifteen, and became four years later, in 1915, a member of the Executive Council of the Norwegian Social Democrat Youth Organisation for which he acted from 1917–19 as vice-chairman. In 1919 he was appointed one of the secretaries to the Norwegian Labour Party, and found time between political meetings to qualify as a barrister.

Two years later, when young Secretary Lie married Hsordis Jorgensen with whom he had grown up, they decided to go to Russia for their honeymoon. Their interest in the New Order was only tempered by the fact that their suitcases were lost and, as it was then impossible to buy new clothes, many meetings had to remain unattended while the young couple waited for their drying laundry.

On his return from Russia in 1922 Lie was appointed Legal Adviser to the Norwegian Trade Unions; a post which he held for thirteen years, and in which he was responsible for winning not only many cases for the employees but the admiration and confidence of their employers. In 1927 he was made a member of the Norwegian Labour Party's executive council, and when Johan Nygaardsvold formed the country's second Labour Government in 1935, Lie was made Minister of Justice.

A convinced feminist, Lie has always opposed discrimination between men and women; women should compete professionally with men: and as Minister of Justice he succeeded in opening more careers to women. A year later he reorganised the Norwegian police force under a unified State control.

Perhaps the greatest single achievement in his career up to that time was his masterly handling of the Profit Sharing Bill in 1938.

In 1939 he accepted the important post of Minister of Supply and Shipping. Realising Norway would have to face a heavy blockade, if not actual war, he concentrated on building up vast supplies in the country, and on 9 April, when the German Minister, Dr Brauer, presented his country's ultimatum to the Government, Norway had greater resources of wheat, coal, rye, and other essential supplies than she ever had in her entire history. On 11 April the King and the Crown Prince and members of the Government were forced, by the deliberate attack of enemy aircraft, to leave Trysil, where they had established themselves; and Minister Lie, together with Minister Wold, accompanied the King and the Crown Prince on their nightmare drive across country to Otta.

The Government assembled at the Stugufaaten Tourist Hotel, high up in Romsdalen, and Lie, still wearing his city suit and galoshes, for he had been unable to find any ski-ing clothes en route that would fit his bulky frame, left for Aandalsnes, where he contacted the British Command. On his return, by a Royal Decree dated 22 April and signed by the King, the Norwegian Government requisitioned all ships, and offered the entire Norwegian fleet to the British and French Governments. On 7 June, when it was clear the British would have to evacuate Norway, the King, the Crown Prince, and members of the Government left on the cruiser *Devonshire* to continue the fight for a free Norway from British soil. Once in London, the

Nygaardsvold Government was broadened by the inclusion of representatives of all parties and took on the character of a National Government; in November Lie became Acting Foreign Minister, a position to which he was officially appointed in February, 1941.

During the occupation, in the Nazi controlled press, Lie was the most feared and attacked member of the Cabinet. His burly shoulders, sturdy walk, and heavy chin lend themselves easily to caricature, and he was often depicted as a ferocious ape or snarling bear. In reality he is a mild mannered man, devoted to his family, and was a genial host to the young Norwegians who crowded his London flat. He loses his temper seldom, and then with great effect, but he has been known to brood for several days if any one of the family should forget his birthday. A passion for anniversaries and football are perhaps the only weaknesses in his character.

A keen sportsman—he was chairman of the Labour Sport Movement in Norway and was responsible for its successful merger with the National Sport Movement in 1940—he is a devoted follower of Chelsea, and could often be found having highly prejudiced discussions on the merits of rival teams with that other great football enthusiast, King Haakon, during their stay in England.

The final word must belong to Norway. On his mission of good-will to Russia, in November of this year, Minister Lie stopped at Stockholm, and one of the questions correspondents asked him was whether he believed, after four years' separation, his Government was still in touch with the people of Norway. 'We are as close to them now as we have ever been both in sympathy and in fact', Lie replied. 'If a bridge is blown we know it over here often before it is known in Norway. If a patriot dies we mourn him often before the news can reach his village. All our energies, and labour, and love are turned towards Norway, and to the day on which we will be united.'

'LITTLE MONTY'
1942

I T is thirty-four years since Bernard Law Montgomery, who is 'little Monty' to his friends, left Sandhurst to join as a subaltern the Royal Warwickshire Regiment, of which, from 1931 to 1934, he was to command a battalion. Ten years of his youth had been spent in Tasmania, where his father was Bishop. He says that the strictness of his religious upbringing left him fed up with 'too much of that sort of thing', and the rigid personal asceticism which is such a feature of his character today does not arise from purely spiritual causes. His keenness for athletics is of long standing; he played 'Rugger' for Sandhurst and hockey for the Army. He is remembered as an exceedingly hardworking young officer, not much interested in the more social activities of the mess. A friend tried to persuade him to take a girl to a dance and chose fittingly, as he thought, the vicar's daughter, whom he invited to tea and seated next to Monty. But, alas, she was discovered both to smoke and drink. Monty pronounced her 'not maidenly' and stayed away from the dance. When later in life, rather to everyone's surprise, he got married, he ruled his household with the authority of a medieval knight. The joyous arrival of a son he treated as a staff problem, and orders for his upbringing and welfare were issued daily. So that when someone asked him if he did not hope for more children, he replied, 'Certainly not. Far too much staff work.'

Montgomery had more than three years on the Western Front during the 1914–18 war, being mentioned six times in despatches and winning the D.S.O. and the French Military Cross. Some say that he was one of those men who had to see too much of warfare, and that it was from his experiences during that time that his eyes got that curious, misty-grey, 'tired' look which so often deceives people into thinking him older than his fifty-four years. Certainly his eyes have seen much. When he lay wounded in No Man's Land another man went out to bring him in. He was hit and fell dead over Montgomery's body. For seven hours the Germans pumped lead into both of them, most of the bullets striking the corpse. As a result, Montgomery lost one lung and owes his life only to the presence of a famous surgeon, who ordered that he should not be touched at the dressing station, but should be sent back to England for special treatment. His physical fitness since is all the more extraordinary.

It was during the years between the wars, at the Staff Colleges at Quetta and Camberley, that Montgomery started working out the system of command which he has retained and improved upon ever since. At that time he called it the fixed battle scheme. In essence it was to ensure that a commander should have the fullest knowledge of what was going on all along the line, and to reduce to a minimum what Clausewitz called the 'friction of war'. Montgomery's system enables him to impose his own battle plan on the enemy. This he has done in both his recent encounters with Rommel. While recently in command of a corps and later an army, Montgomery, by constant training and manoeuvres gathered the lessons which have made him the equal of Rommel in experience. Mistakes were often made, but he never allowed them to be made twice. In manoeuvres he would be followed by two of his staff officers on motor cycles, whom he would order to take down the name of any officer who had distinguished himself either by success or failure. He struck the fear of God into many. He was often brusque and rude, but never sarcastic. 'You're good, Mr So-and-so, but you're not good enough', he would say to an officer he was going to sack. On entering his H.Q. one would be confronted with a notice: Three Questions of the Day. (1) Are you 100 per cent fit? (2) Are you 100 per cent up to your job? (3) Are you 100 per cent full of *binge*?

Binge was the name of several of his exercises and was a pet word of his. No one knows why, for the nearest Monty has ever got to what others call a binge is to go to the piano and sing *Little Brown Jug*, polishing off the performance with a glass of water. Actually he seems to use the word binge in its more Edwardian sense of punch, zip, or just 'guts'. He gave a rude jolt to officers and men who were comfortably combining a little domestic ease with their military duties by ordering all wives out of areas under his command. Coming on top of the six-mile a week run for all ranks under forty this was too much of a good thing for some.

Like Joffre, Montgomery retires to bed by ten and rises at five. But there the resemblance ends. He is a hard thinker and a quick thinker. He can retain enormously intricate staff problems in his head. In fact, he boasted that in France, in 1940 he never had to write an order. He believes in making himself absolutely clear to his officers. It is said that immediately on arrival in the desert he addressed all his officers, ignoring protests that some must not be taken from the front line in order to attend. 'N.C.O.s should be perfectly competent to take over, after two years in the field', he is reported to have replied.

Monty is a 100 per cent professional soldier. His only ambition is to do the job as well as possible. To him this just means hard work. As well as stupendous mental alertness he has that infinite capacity for taking pains in all matters, big or small. He has, too, the great quality, essential in a good general, of robustness of temperament. Because of his hard thinking, he he is not easily surprised, and his serenity in the dangerous moment when his preparations for the offensive were interrupted by Rommel's attack seemed to eradicate the word 'flap' from the desert vocabulary. But, above all, he believes in that maxim of Ardant du Picq that 'the Man is the first weapon of battle'. Every man, whatever his trade or speciality (cook, clerk, driver or signaller), is a soldier first. Every man knows his job in the team. He is the first British general who can say 'The Army and the Air Arm are operationally one'. His faith in the British soldier was rewarded with a famous victory for British arms. To Monty and his Army fell the honour of destroying for ever the legend of German invincibility.

VICEROYS

LORD WAVELL

EVEN at the best of times there can be few positions so lonely as that of Viceroy of India. Never can it have been so lonely or so anxious as during Lord Wavell's term. He is a man whose story has been one of continual summons, to claw ship after ship from off lee shores.

Archibald Percival Wavell (born in 1883) joined The Black Watch from Winchester, where he was a scholar, by way of Sandhurst in 1901. He arrived in South Africa for the tail-end of the war, and went on to India. In those days he had no fixed intention of taking the Army seriously. He decided to sit for the Staff College on a sudden impulse, when a brother officer whom he was trying to lure on to the polo field declined on the ground that he was working for Camberley. Two or three months before his own exam, Wavell was obliged by his commanding officer to take leave in order to cram: most of it he spent shooting bear in the Himalayas, before going home and passing easily.

After Camberley he spent two years with the Russian Army before going to the War Office. In the first World War he served for two years in France, losing an eye at Loos; and then, because of his knowledge of Russia, he was sent to join the Grand Duke Nicholas in the Caucasus. From there he went to Allenby in Palestine, a chance to which we owe one of the best military biographies ever written.

The writing of the life of Allenby, in its two parts, aptly illustrates one of Lord Wavell's most distinctive gifts: his power of concentration in the midst of distraction. The second volume was written in 1940 and 1941, when Lord Wavell was performing his own most remarkable feats of arms in North Africa. Even as Viceroy, he found relaxation in writing, or rather in dictating; and the days are rare when he neither rides a horse nor plays nine holes of golf. No man ever managed his leisure better, or made less heavy weather of it.

History will assuredly acclaim as classic his handling of tiny resources in those desert campaigns. His soldiers of those early days, when you meet them now in London, cleaning windows or conducting buses, burst out in pride at having belonged to that small but honoured army. Their trust in him remained unshaken even when that army, which had so often accomplished the seemingly impossible, was finally ordered to attempt the truly impossible; when, virtually unreinforced and weakened by Greece and Crete and the Western Desert, Lord Wavell was bidden to undertake simultaneous campaigns in Syria, Iraq, and the Western Desert again. Two of these succeeded and one failed; and in July of 1941 he went with dignity to India, exchanging commands with General Auchinleck.

Five months later Japan was in the war, and Lord Wavell was commanding against her. His resources now were far smaller even than they had been in Egypt.

In South-East Asia he was called in when the show was already in a mess, and with a vista of hopelessly lean years ahead. Altogether, in the late war, he fought close on a dozen campaigns with never a Court card in his hand. Yet, if the war treated him harshly in this respect, it left his military reputation standing high, and in many ways justified his remarkable foresight. Much military thought which today is normal was unorthodox 'Wavellism' ten years ago.

In June, 1943, Wavell's appointment as Viceroy was announced. As a student of history he must have known that India has wrecked more reputations than it has made. Only a year earlier, as Commander-in-Chief, it had been his unenviable task to suppress a civil rebellion. On Lord Linlithgow fell most of the opprobrium for the harsh measures that had to be adopted; but Lord Wavell was inevitably involved. That the memory of these bitter days faded fast speaks eloquently for the man. Many of the Congress rebel leaders who were imprisoned in the '42 disturbances became three years later Lord Wavell's Ministers of State.

LORD WAVELL

Unlike his predecessors, Lord Wavell took practical steps to show his sympathy with India's political aspirations, and made no fuss about it. Too often in the past, during crises, Viceroys had governed aloofly from Delhi; not Lord Wavell. His dramatic flying visit to Calcutta at the height of the Bengal famine, his energetic spurring of the slothful official machine that had allowed thousands to die unnecessarily, are still remembered with gratitude.

The annual exodus to Simla, summer headquarters of the Government of India, curtailed by his predecessor, ceased altogether when he took over. The pomp and glitter of viceregal life were drastically reduced. When the scale of the Bengal famine became known, Lord Wavell set the country a much-needed example of austere living. Meals, even official banquets, were cut to a skeleton. The vast sweep of viceregal lawns was ploughed under to raise fine crops of wheat, maize, and vegetables.

The widespread public affection which Lord Wavell earned in India owes nothing to his powers of speech: he is no orator and has no aptitude for small-talk. With intimates he can talk brilliantly and entertainingly; but even with intimates he can be tongue-tied. To his staff and subordinates he is accessible and not alarming; his favourite phrase is a slow and thoughtful 'I see'. As Commander-in-Chief he liked to stand at a tall desk to look at the map and stroke his chin for minutes at a time; then, with sudden energy, he would turn, say 'Come on', and be into his car or on to his horse briskly and away.

Physically, he is immensely fit. He has had his fair share of accidents; he has had many falls from a horse, and once at Singapore during the war he fell over a quayside in the dark and broke two ribs. One of the first generals to exploit flying as a normal means of travel, he has the reputation of a Jonah in the air: no V.I.P. has such a record of forced landings.

His task in India was heavy and thankless, and success eluded him. But he pursued his work of reconciliation quietly and undeterred; patience is his long suit. From few of her sons has Britain asked so much, and from none has she had more ungrudging and faithful service.

EARL MOUNTBATTEN

EARL MOUNTBATTEN, the last Viceroy of all India and the first Governor-General of the partitioned Dominion of India, returned to England with a singular reputation. He is still a relatively young man—rising forty-eight—and everyone wondered what high office he would next be offered.

The peculiarity of his reputation is that it has always symbolised success. Away back in the 'twenties he emerged, a handsome youth, royal, wealthy, athletic, and happy, a secondary version of his friend and elder cousin, the then Prince of Wales, who was, of course, the idol of the people.

Lord and Lady Louis Mountbatten, with their fabulous penthouse flat in Park Lane, their travels, their parties and their friends, were success itself to most newspaper readers. But not to them only. In the Navy he had a sound professional reputation as a most energetic and inventive signals officer, which means wireless and gadgets, and he achieved undoubted success when he became the youngest Captain in the Service. To his intimates he was not only more authentically gay than his somewhat shy cousin, but he was also impressive by his ability to overcome difficulties—playing polo well without natural talent, for example—and by a certain originality of mind. This was chiefly evident in his taste for heterodox views, including mildly political ones, which always had this in common, that they were new and up to date.

The declaration of war in 1939—it was his second; he had served as a young officer in three classes of ship, including submarines in the first World War—was to give him his real chance. He rose to the challenge of physical strain and danger like the real hero that he is. For the first two and a half years of the struggle he saw as much active service as any man of his rank could. His feats—they were real feats, not routine operations—were more thrilling than any novelist's invention, and were characterised not only by great boldness but also by nobility and generosity.

His courageous and skilful naval operations can be criticised on grounds of judgment: it has been pointed out that his successes often involved the disablement of his ship. But they proved one thing beyond doubt, that he possessed in a very high degree the qualities of leadership, which means inspiring others to do what they otherwise would not.

In those hushed and lonely years of our grim struggle to survive, little or no publicity was given to any individual actions; and Mountbatten did not become famous until Churchill appointed him to be Chief of Combined Operations in May, 1942. That summer was the turning point of the war, and Mountbatten's name became not merely symbolic but almost synonymous with success. The Combined Operations Command meant two things—Commando raids on the coasts of Europe and the experimental training for amphibious invasion; that is to say, the prelude and preparations for the final victorious assault. No one could have encouraged audacity in attack and inventiveness in technique more ably than Mountbatten.

His success in this phase must, however, be qualified by the failure of his largest scale operation, the Dieppe raid, although if his judgment was at fault, so were those of Churchill, Montgomery, and MacNaughton, who presumably endorsed his operational plan.

Next came his appointment as Supreme Allied Commander, South-East Asia Command. This raised him to the highest level of military command, the level which approaches statesmanship. Indeed, there was said to be a political consideration in his appointment—his outstanding acceptability to the Americans, who by this time were bulking large in the Western war effort. But why should he have been particularly *bien vu* by the Americans? The answer is chiefly that he likes them and, to a surprising extent, is like them—the terrific energy, the taste for new ideas and new methods, the social informality and lack of stuffiness, and the confidence and belief in success, all these characteristics he shares with them.

And so it was MacArthur and Mountbatten who directed the war against the Japanese. Mountbatten had the worst of the territory and MacArthur had first call on what men and supplies were not already engaged in Europe. The vast and gloomy jungles of Burma, stretching over a territory as wide as half Europe and pestilentially unhealthy—how on earth could one be successful on such a terrain? He set up the most up-to-date headquarters at Kandy in Ceylon: he took out all his henchmen; and he went to work inspiring his troops, planning fantastic strategems and conciliating as best he could his neighbouring Commander in China, 'Vinegar Joe' Stilwell.

The atom bombs on Hiroshima and Nagasaki ended this huge and grim drama, but not before Mountbatten's troops had had to fight horrifying battles at Kohima and Imphal. At once, and for nine extraordinary months, he was plunged into a new rôle, that of *de facto* ruler of all South-East Asia, an area inhabited by 128,000,000 discomfited and disorganised human beings. It was a political baptism by total immersion, and a man of more profound knowledge and more prudent judgment would probably not have come to the surface at all. But with buoyancy and verve, he went straight for the obvious and the unorthodox: he came to terms with Aung Sang, the revolutionary leader of the Burmese resistance. It was a gamble, and it more or less came off. The Dutch East Indies proved even harder to cope with. Whether the decisions taken at that time in both these countries were inevitable and whether they were sound are debatable questions.

When the professional administrators took over, Mountbatten withdrew; reappeared in London, rested; and for a spell it was not plain what would become of him. He was appointed to command a Cruiser Squadron in the Mediterranean. Suddenly the Labour Government asked him to succeed Wavell as the Viceroy who would end the British Raj in India and speed the now inevitable partition of that immense, distracted subcontinent, with its teeming millions of muddlers and malcontents and pathetic sufferers. At once Mountbatten was heralded anew as the man of the hour.

But how could he succeed in India, the cemetery of reputations, and in this awful transitional period? Undaunted and this time largely unaccompanied by henchmen, he set off for

Government House, New Delhi. And partition was pressed through at the gallop. The Indian princes, who were forlorn and recalcitrant, were told by this super prince that they simply had to lump it, and they did. Some hasty misjudgments occurred over Kashmir, but the job was pushed on and through. Today, there is Pakistan, and there is India, and there has been no major civil war. Who can say that this broad result would have been achieved by less dynamic and more prudent means?

His experiences in Asia have certainly matured him. They have also given further evidence of his special quality, his authentic power of leadership, this time exercised in supremely difficult circumstances. Remarkable tributes were paid him, such as that by his successor-designate, Mr Rajagopalachari. 'Indians recognise charm as a quality of the heart.' How many of our public figures could convince even us, let alone Indians, that they have either charm or heart?

His future—one can only guess. It need not be feared that he is wildly ambitious. He has a certain quality of disinterestedness about the big things. Probably, his instinct will be to go down to the sea again, and to escape the honorific type of post to which his royal birth has always made him liable.

It might be well if he were allowed to go back to the sea. It would give him time to think, and it would keep him available for the sort of post to which his gifts are best suited. For instance, if ever a Commander-in-Chief of all three Services were considered a modern necessity, he would have strong professional credentials for such a post, and it would draw on exactly that quality of his success which is the most real, consistent, and rare. His correct employment is undoubtedly in the leading of men, either in work or in action, rather than in politics or diplomacy.

GENERAL ROBERTSON

GENERAL SIR BRIAN ROBERTSON is the most powerful man in the British Control Commission for Germany—in fact, though not in name, Viceroy of a quarter of Germany. He has won this power by great ability in a very exacting position.

Berlin from 1945 to 1948 was the microcosm of Europe, the meeting point of East and West. Nowhere was conflict more apparent; nowhere agreement more imperative. Against a background of conflicting Great Power interests, quadripartite Government had to be carried on from day to day. There was no escape into generalities and saving formulas, as sometimes in diplomatic conferences; the ever-present alternative to precise and specific agreed decisions was administrative breakdown. It was a tough job for a simple soldier to face. But then, General Robertson is not a simple soldier.

The son of Field-Marshal Sir William Robertson—the first Field-Marshal to rise from the ranks—he was, of course, brought up in the Army. He was a cadet at Sandhurst in 1914, he served with distinction as a subaltern throughout the first World War, and he stayed on in the Army afterwards. But at thirty-seven, in 1933—the year his father died—he suddenly retired from the Army and decided to become a business man.

The offer he had was to become assistant manager in South Africa of the Dunlop Rubber Company. He reasoned simply and clearly that if there was no war in the near future the Army would offer him nothing like such scope for initiative and responsibility; and if there was a war the Army would want him back anyhow. That settled it. It was the first time Robertson showed what has since struck many people as his perhaps most outstanding characteristic: a rare capacity for making up his mind.

So the regular soldier Major Robertson gave way to Sir Brian Robertson, rubber magnate. He was Dunlop's chief manager in South Africa within a year, and he made a brilliant success of that job. There is no indication that during the following six years he gave the Army a thought.

GENERAL ROBERTSON

The war brought him back. He joined the South African Army, was posted to Ethiopia, 'discovered' by General Cunningham, and made Chief Administrative Officer of the Eighth Army when Cunningham became its Commander. Robertson's appointment proved more permanent than Cunningham's own. He remained the 'manager' of the Eighth Army under all its many Commanders, finishing the war as Alexander's Chief Administrative Officer in Sicily and Italy.

By the time he was appointed Chief of Staff in Germany under Montgomery in 1945, he had had almost every type of experience this strange job demanded. His work in South Africa had given him understanding of economic problems; it had also taught him how to negotiate across a table. His year in Italy had given him experience in the administration of a defeated and disrupted country. His standing with the military was guaranteed by his Regular Army background and his brilliant Eighth Army reputation. He had also had a taste of international diplomacy in his earlier Army life when he had served as a junior member of the British Mission of Military Experts to the Disarmament Conference at Geneva.

The authority which these qualifications give him is enhanced by a dominating personality. He is a tall, slender man, always wearing battle dress. He has the colouring of the typical Scot—thinning sandy hair, and penetrating blue eyes under bushy brows. His pale face is paler now with strain, and the set of his upper lip is firm and obstinate. It is a strong reserved face, strangely veiled with shyness. He can laugh, but does not do so often. He is slow-smiling, slow-moving, seldom completely at ease. He does not suffer fools gladly, and in Berlin he has developed something of the reputation of a man-eating tiger. Several high-ranking officers have found themselves posted away from Berlin overnight. This has generated an atmosphere of fear around the General. But he is, as people of this type often are, capable of inspiring devotion. Those working closely with him in his inner team speak with shining eyes of his seriousness and simplicity, his complete objectivity, his quick grasp, and his power of decision.

Robertson is, however, at his best in Conference, whether as Chairman or as exponent of the British view. He easily dominates a meeting. Taking a complex brief with ease, equipped with a spacious memory, adroit in using any advantageous opening in debate, perfectly self-controlled, determined, persevering, but always ready to suggest the workable compromise, he may claim much of the credit for the astonishing amount of practical agreements which were again and again wrested from fundamental disagreement in Berlin.

It is true that the agreements were seldom fully satisfactory, and sometimes frankly deplorable. The most frequent, and perhaps the most telling, criticism of Robertson is that the diplomatist in him got the better of the administrator, and that in saving for such a long time quadripartite Government, and thereby a slender hope of German unity, he sometimes came dangerously near to jeopardising the physical needs of existence of the British Zone.

For three fateful years, General Robertson has, as Britain's chief representative in Germany, been making history. All the time, his name has remained all but unknown to the wider public. He prefers it that way. But, if free from vanity, he is not necessarily free from ambition—an objective ambition which aims at results rather than fame.

GENERAL CLAY

WHEN General Clay went to Germany in 1945 to become America's Chief Administrator there, the *Washington Post* commented acidly: 'General Clay's exceedingly high abilities are better suited to the German situation than to our own. . . . That task calls for authoritarianism.' Much later, a British high official in Germany was heard to remark on him, after a hard bargaining session: 'He looks like a Roman Emperor—and acts like one.'

It would be misreading these comments to regard them as a reflection on General Clay's political convictions. Nobody could have less sympathy for despotism. The son of a Southern Senator of the 'reconstruction' period after the American civil war, Lucius Clay inherited an unquestioning, indeed a fundamentalist, belief in parliamentary democracy of the American model as the perfect form of Government; with it went a strong, deep-seated anti-centralist bias, a Southern Confederate sympathy for individual State rights against central authority. Both these beliefs are strongly stamped on General Clay's work in Germany.

But his democratic convictions are served by an autocratic temperament, and by a technocratic mind. Observers of his rule as American Military Governor sometimes feel that he handles the creation of a democratic Germany as something like an engineering operation, with himself at the controls. The operation has been spectacular, and in a way it has been successful. But the success has a somewhat brittle brilliance.

By career General Clay is an Army engineer. In the war, he was for two years Assistant Chief of Staff for Materials; then, after personally organising the supply base at Cherbourg during the Normandy invasion, for the last half-year Mr Byrnes's Deputy as Director of War Mobilisation. All these were back-room jobs, but colossal back-room jobs; General Clay was one of the few men at the mainswitch of American power. At the same time, he was never responsible for political decisions. He was responsible for execution—and he was a brilliant executive, single-minded, hard-working, ruthless. He got results. He made a reputation. And he made enemies.

One must see all this in perspective—the democratic orthodoxy and the Southern anti-centralism as well as the somewhat mechanical logic of the engineer's and technocrat's mind, the fierce will-power and the ruthless insistence on results, as well as the executive's habit 'not to reason why'. Only thus can we understand General Clay's impressive and controversial career in Germany.

It is a career full of contradictions and paradoxes, of which the biggest is perhaps that this is outwardly the most successful attempt ever made to impose democracy by command. The smoke had hardly cleared from the South German battlefields when the General began to establish the outward paraphernalia of democracy—parties, advisory assemblies, provisional local governments. Against the advice of nearly all his officials, General Clay held local elections in the American Zone half a year after the surrender; five months later the new South German *Lands* of his creation had their Constituent Assemblies. In the summer of 1946, when the rest of Germany had hardly begun to emerge from utter chaos, the American Zone looked a neat little model Confederacy. This is nothing to scoff at; it is a magnificent achievement of political engineering. But it is not the way in which the genuine and durable democracies of the world have come into being.

It is probably true that General Clay really had his heart in this creation of his South German Confederacy. And it is a nice historical irony that eighty years after the almost simultaneous defeat of the American Confederate South at the hands of Lincoln, and of the German Confederate South at the hands of Bismarck, a son of Georgia should have his revenge in Bavaria.

But for the rest, General Clay was, and is, in Germany, as before in Washington, the brilliant and ardent executant of policy decisions which were not his. He had to denazify, demilitarise, decentralise, democratise—and nowhere were these four 'de's' executed with a more vigorous technical efficiency and a more resounding statistical success. The trouble was that these policy directives, perhaps not entirely compatible from the start, became increasingly contradictory as time went on and American high policy changed. General Clay came with a Morgenthau brief of destruction. He stayed to execute a Marshall brief of reconstruction—but with many of his political directives unrevised. The resulting impression was sometimes one of schizophrenia; and American administration occasionally appeared to the onlooker like a magnificent high-powered car, with the front and back wheels turning at full speed in opposite directions.

However, the general trend of American administration was from harshness towards benevolence, and it would be unjust to attribute this change entirely to stratospheric developments in Washington. General Clay had his personal share in it. There seems to be a kind of political law by which Military Governors turn gradually into advocates of the countries they are supposed to keep down. General Clay has conformed to that law with even greater vehemence than others.

As a person, the General is impressive, but far from simple; he evades summing-up. Slim, medium height, dark bushy eyebrows, thin features, aquiline nose, deep-socketed eyes, a piercing glance, and a deliberate smile—that is how he meets you. He speaks with a slow, soft voice, smoking one cigarette after another, with a patient charm that does not entirely hide stubbornness and a capacity for quick bursts of temper. He has an alert mind, with a rapid grasp of essentials, and a penetrating intelligence, but no broad vision and little intellectual sensitivity. Businesslike and unpompous, hard-working, a strict disciplinarian, he is respected rather than liked by his staff. He is fiery or cold, not warm. But he is an immensely capable and completely honest man, acting with devastating efficiency, in accordance with his orders, but also with sincerely-held ideals and convictions.

In three years he has, outwardly at any rate, changed part of an old historic country of Europe beyond recognition. Few men can boast to have done anything like that, whether it lasts or not.

FIRST LADIES
AND LEADING LADIES

MRS ROOSEVELT

IT is well known in America that Roosevelts are always a law unto themselves. Eleanor Roosevelt is no exception to this rule, though it has taken her longer than most to prove it. Her mother died when she was ten years old and she at once became used to having to fend for herself since she had to look after her younger brother, Hall Roosevelt, which earned her the nickname of 'Granny'. She had few friends, and her shyness made her dread the rare Roosevelt family gatherings which she had to attend, full of terrifying cousins and aunts like the handsome and forbidding Mrs James Roosevelt, whose son Franklin, however, an eighth cousin, usually seemed to go out of his way to be nice to her. At sixteen she took it into her head to go to England and attend finishing school, got permission, and went.

The head of the school soon saw that this intelligent, but unsure, girl would develop with encouragement, and she did her best to draw her out of her shell, both at school and when they spent the holidays together touring in Europe. This independent-minded old lady, with her outspokenly pro-Boer views voiced in the midst of the war, started Eleanor off on a path of liberalism and social service which she was never to abandon.

While abroad she had hoped that her remote cousin had not altogether forgotten her. Nor had he, much to the concern of old Mrs Roosevelt, who packed him off on a West Indian cruise to forget or, as she put it, to be sure of his mind. This he most certainly was, and though he pretended during the cruise that she was no longer uppermost in his thoughts, they soon found themselves engaged and then married. The devoted husband became aware, too, that she was the favourite niece of Theodore Roosevelt. They both received a good idea of the importance of politics at their wedding: the guests abandoned the bride and bridegroom to listen to the 'President's killing stories'.

Eleanor Roosevelt says that the first ten years of her married life were spent entirely in preparing for or recovering from the births of her six children.

She also says that it took her a considerable part of this time to understand what married life meant and to acquire the rudiments of a sense of humour, which was something she had conspicuously lacked. Her chief preoccupation was something called 'good works'. 'A certain kind of orthodox goodness was my ideal and ambition.' She used to be afraid that Franklin would turn out too much of a cynic or a dilettante and was hurt by his cheerful amusement at her worries over the children's religious education, a subject which he didn't consider worth any loss of sleep. She had not yet begun to follow very closely Franklin's political career. 'I understood little about the fight for Wilson's nomination, though my husband I knew was deeply interested . . .' and, indeed, politics up till 1918 were more of an enemy, the thing that kept her from laying eyes on Franklin, and which made family life difficult. Looking back on that attitude she says, 'I wonder how they bore with me in those days. I had no sense of values whatsoever.'

It was during Franklin's unsuccessful Vice-Presidential campaign on the League of Nations platform that she began to play a considerable part. It was 'Louie' Howe, that extraordinary little Albany journalist, wizened, unkempt and indispensable, who tutored her in the customs and standards of American pressmen and politicians and in the duties of a candidate's wife.

Then came the sudden incredible blow that changed both their lives. Franklin was stricken with infantile paralysis. She put everything into the struggle to get him well. She understood better than his mother that he would never be able to endure the existence of an invalid, so much did he depend on the stimulus of friends and the excitement of political life. During the eight years of his illness, aided by 'Louie' Howe, she kept up his interest and took over much of his work. She became a member of the Women's Trade Union League. Although still fearful of her political ignorance she presided over the Women's Democratic Committee and the League of Women's Voters. She had to fight back her distaste of many aspects of the life. She learnt to speak well, briefly, and to the point. But the main task was to keep Franklin going. He had said 'I'll beat this thing'. When partial victory was won at last, she merely claimed that 'we didn't do anything except treat him as a normal able-bodied man, which is what he made us all feel he was.'

From then on, her self-confidence was complete and her public life became increasingly important. Yet when they moved to the White House in 1933 it became more important than she could imagine, both for herself and for the President. Washington and the nation were used to First Ladies being rarely seen and never heard. Some of the President's advisers were worried. She ignored them and seemed to say:

> Ah, look not thus on me
> So grave and sad
> Shake not your heads nor say the lady's mad.

Charles Francis Adams had complained that a very different President's wife, Mary Lincoln, 'had got hold of newspaper reporters and railroad conductors as the best persons to go to for advice and direction'. Eleanor Roosevelt did more than this. She established such warm and personal contacts all over the length and breadth of the United States that she proved an invaluable adviser to a President forced to remain in the Federal capital. During the difficult years of the New Deal, when the Roosevelts' own class pushed its opposition to the point of the filthiest personal abuse of the couple in the White House, Eleanor Roosevelt was able to make the reassuring discovery that the President was unpopular with everybody save a great majority of the electors.

Her newspaper column, *My Day*, became more and more a place where she could say what she pleased without regard to the official feelings of the Administration. She slammed at the dictators, at appeasement; above all, she defended the young, yet urged them to look further and more unselfishly ahead. She is the common-sense woman of America only she has more common sense, more honesty, and more real 'heart' than most. She has long ago given up thinking of herself and of her own problems. 'If you *could* by way of change think of yourself', wrote her husband from the war zone in 1917. She has more energy than any woman in the world. 'She never stopped writing or talking', said a train attendant.

'I had a great curiosity about life and a desire to participate in every experience that might be the lot of woman. There seemed to be a necessity for hurry.' She wrote that a long time ago. She hasn't changed her mind about it.

SEÑORA PERÓN

'OUR century will not be known as the century of the world wars, not even as the century of atomic energy, but as the century of triumphant feminism.' Thus Eva Perón in a broadcast from Madrid during her more than regal progress through Spain and on to the Vatican.

What an outing it was, of a lavishness and *panache* altogether unheard-of in our drab days. And who was the heroine of Franco's somewhat hectic version of a royal reception? A young woman of humble origin who has risen from almost nothing to the dizziest heights of world-wide publicity in little more than a couple of years.

It is of course her own triumph that is meant when she proclaims the century of 'triumphant feminism'. In her ringing voice there is pride, challenge, victorious boast, quivering ambition. But she seldom actually speaks of herself. This extravagantly dressed young woman uses the language of a story-book revolutionary, invariably addressing herself to the poor, as if her triumph somehow avenged their poverty.

Señora Perón's career is usually discussed by the knowing in terms of anecdotes and piquant rumours: they say she is the *éminence rose* of Argentina. Looks, charm, audacity—of course, they are all there. But they are not unique to her and do not explain her popular success in her country, which is authentic. There are dozens of *provincianitas*, poor but lovely young girls from farms and villages who make their way to Buenos Aires every year in pursuit of adventure and happiness. A few make bourgeois marriages, some a living on the stage, but most end in the hospital for poor people.

Maria Eva Duarte, the daughter of a poor farm labourer, arrived in the capital of Argentina not many years ago, scarcely knowing a soul. But this was no ordinary *provincianita*. It was a girl of boundless self-confidence and vitality who cared for more than a stage career or even a bourgeois marriage.

Nor did the ambitious politician Perón pick her up by chance and make her famous. She was already famous in Argentina when they met. First she had tried the stage and

SEÑORA PERÓN

screen and become a minor star, but her artistry was not great and her personality too direct for acting. Then she went to the radio and there, where it is not a matter of looks, she succeeded. Her personality—warm, vibrant, witty, and emotionally generous—got across and home to the masses who listen in. For millions of Argentinos she became 'Señorita Radio'. And so it was that she was one of the persons of nation-wide popularity on whom Colonel Perón, not yet in full power, called in 1942 when he wanted to make a sensational appeal for a national fund for earthquake victims. That was how they met, as two sincere and successful exponents of glamour demagogy.

Perón is famous for his many romantic affairs. Why should this particular friendship have lasted and become formalised, where so many had faded and passed? The answer might just be feminine artfulness. But Señorita Duarte would surely not still have been single if to 'catch your man' had been her main idea. Such a forceful, self-made young woman must have turned down many marriage propositions which, from her origins, looked good enough. No, the less scandalous truth is that when Evita met Perón it was a meeting of twin souls. Both were highly energetic and ambitious, with a love of adventure, drama and success. But, above all, both adored popularity and had the same feeling as to how it could be won.

Sincerely possessed, indeed infatuated, by their idea, they set out to make the Argentinos happy by making themselves beloved of them. Their appeal was simply that they were against the very rich and the U.S.A., for the poor and Argentina. Their struggle, although short, was not entirely uneventful. In October, 1945, when Perón momentarily fell from power and was arrested, it was 'Señorita Radio' who came to his rescue—rallying his adherents, agitating, plotting, arranging meetings, and, in the end, herself passing the order for that general strike which brought Perón smiling out of gaol and immensely helped him to be voted into his dictatorship.

A female radio star who calls a general strike that changes a régime. What a fantastic successor to the women of the *directoire*, to Madame Tallien and Josephine Beauharnais! Yet this warm-hearted and peroxided peasant's daughter claims descent from these revolutionaries of more momentous ideas by always using the phrases of revolution—although she has since become the wife of General Perón and First Lady of one of the richest and most exuberant of countries in an impoverished world.

Eva Perón—'twenty-seven to her friends, thirty-two to her enemies', but in any case still young and in full flower—has arrived. Will she now change and settle down to the routine of political success and social eminence? So far, the indications are that she will not. More highly dressed and richly bejewelled than the most elegant ladies of Buenos Aires society, she yet refuses to become one of them. She prefers to remind them continually that she is of the people—and to hear the people's still unabated applause. When asked to become the patron of a highly exclusive charitable society, she publicly refused and recommended them to invite her mother instead—a humble working woman from an obscure Pampas village. Wrapped in furs and sparkling with diamonds, she still addresses the workers of Buenos Aires as one of them: '*Nosotros los descamisados*'—We the Shirtless. And in Argentina, if not in Europe, she gets away with it. To her own people, those from whom she sprang, she is a dream come true, Cinderella become Queen. And just as a rather famous tyrant, recently deceased, continued when all-powerful to refer to himself as the simple soldier of the trenches, so Evita, although enthroned, still feels herself to be the representative of all those who sweep the cinders. Her legend is factually the less untrue of the two.

Any comparison between the régime of Perón and the Fascist régimes of the Old World should take note of one important difference. Argentina is rich, whereas the countries of the former Axis were poor. Hitler, Mussolini and Franco came to power and ruled with violence in an atmosphere of tragedy, but Perón . . . he smiles, laughs, calls for rejoicing and uses violence very sparingly. There are no deeply bitter hatreds in a country so affluent as Argentina. You only have to share out some of the proceeds of the immensely lucrative beef trade to make your dictatorship a real success at the sole cost of

SEÑORA PERÓN

annoying a few millionaires and, of course, of nauseating the civilised and sincere democrats amongst the intelligentsia. And so Eva Perón may be excused for mistaking herself for the darling of the world. If to say in heartfelt tones that you are the friend of the shirtless, while possessing a wardrobe requiring a special plane to transport it, sounds to European ears naïve, theatrical and either offensive or pleasantly diverting, it is music to the millions in Argentina. To us, the Fascist salute means a nightmare that happened. To Señora Perón, it evidently seems just a gesture in a great show, the theme of which is: 'Poor Girl makes Good and is loved by one and all for ever and ever.'

NINETTE DE VALOIS

ENGLISH ballet, not more than sixteen years old, has, in a manner of speaking, found its billet. Ballet used to be an exotic entertainment for the 'arty' and exquisite few. Now it is everybody's pleasure and causes box-office fever on tour as in London.

In her mid-'teens Miss de Valois, billed as 'the miniature Pavlova', toured English seaside resorts with a troupe of Wonder Children. ('I have danced the Dying Swan on every pier in the British Isles', she exults.) In the Sadler's Wells ballet company the ex-Wonder Child cradled and nurtured a Wonder Child of her own.

She was summoned to the task by the late Lilian Baylis in the late 'twenties, first putting on curtain-raiser ballets at the Old Vic and devising ingredient dances for opera and plays. She worked with a scratch company, rehearsing in odd corners, including dressing rooms and theatre bars. All the time her hopes were fixed on splendours remote.

Her chance came in January, 1931, with the opening of Sadler's Wells as Miss Baylis's twin theatre. At the outset Miss de Valois was allowed one ballet evening per fortnight. She soon burst these narrow bonds. The theatre was not a success as a second lodging for the Bard: but his place was taken by song and dance and Sadler's Wells was the real fountain of the new English ballet. The de Valois ballet school found the talent and schooled it. A skilfully planned repertory drew the public; and the public, in its turn, stimulated further enterprise in programme-planning. From being an appendage, the Sadler's Wells ballet, now headquartered at Covent Garden, with one foot remaining in Rosebery Avenue, became a self-sufficing entity.

Ballet mistress became director; a creator as well as general inspirer and administrator. Her achievements as choreographer are hardy, enduring: history will tell of them. When the curtain fell on the dress rehearsal of *Job*, danced to Vaughan Williams's music, she wanted to walk away quickly into the night without a word to anybody, convinced that her share of the work was a nauseous flop. Bit by bit it dawned upon her that she had helped to create a masterpiece. Everybody said so. Everybody says so to this day. She is still slightly incredulous, but bows before universal testimony.

Afterwards came collaboration with Gavin Gordon and the late Rex Whistler in *The Rake's Progress*. When this work first elated and delighted the Wells public one felt in the marrow of one's bones that here was no homespun, parochial thing; clearly one was in the presence of a European asset. This conviction has since been amply ratified by the enthusiasm which the *Rake* aroused in Paris, Brussels, Vienna, Berlin.

It is not too much to say that Miss de Valois is the English equivalent of Serge Diaghilev. She danced for Diaghilev during her formative years. There has been no aping or echoing of the Great Boyar of the *Ballets Russe*. She saw him clearly, assessed him precisely and admiringly; then went her own way, which was independent of his, although parallel to it.

To understand her Sadler's Wells creation in the round it is necessary to look at Miss de Valois's career from the nursery up. De Valois is not her real name but a professional label of her mother's choosing which dates from the Wonder Children days. She comes of an Anglo-Irish family which had a seat two miles outside Blessington in the Wicklow Hills. Her father, Lt-Col. Stannus, D.S.O., of the Leinster Regiment, was killed in the 1914–18 war. On his side there was a French Huguenot strain; on the maternal side a touch of Scots through her great-grandmother, Elizabeth Grant, author of *Memoirs of a Highland Lady*.

When Edris Stannus, the future choreographer, was eight the family settled in England. What more natural than that Edris should be sent to Mrs Wordsworth's dancing class in South Kensington? Did not every little girl in London go to Mrs Wordsworth? There was no notion of a stage future, of course. The family tradition on both sides was Navy and Army and everything belonging. But Edris suddenly awoke to the fact that dancing was a beckoning, imperative vocation.

A spell at a children's theatrical school was followed, at the age of fifteen, by the Wonder Children tour and by selection as

OBSERVER PROFILES

principal dancer for the 1914–15 pantomime at the Lyceum, where she danced annually in Christmas shows throughout the war. She mounted a variety act, danced among other places at the old Oxford, and toured a provincial circuit.

In those days the tradition of hearty barbarity still prevailed at the second 'house' on Monday night—and a ballet turn was prime game for gallery rowdies. Miss de Valois, who specialises in modest over-statement, says, 'Not only have I danced on every pier. I have also been hissed off every music hall stage in England'. There was a particularly memorable night of pandemonium at the Liverpool Empire. Ninette could not hear a note of the music. 'Why don't you bring the curtain down?' she asked. 'We never bring the curtain down until they begin throwing things', said the manager, who knew the rules and was sticking to them.

Lessons with Espinosa and, for five years, with the legendary Cechetti at his place in Shaftesbury Avenue. . . . Dancing in opera at the first post-war international season at Covent Garden. . . . Nineteen-nineteen was the end of an epoch. Gala night programmes for the Royal box were printed on satin for the last time. When the bell rang in the ballet room and it was time for the dancers to go on the stage, the Belgian ballet master picked up his silver-knobbed cane, put on his gloves and bowler hat as though for the street, and, thus accoutred, watched with a merciless eye from the prompt wing. . . .

Then the years with Diaghilev, 1923–25: Paris, Barcelona, Monte Carlo, The Hague, London, Berlin, Munich. They were unmatchable years of enervating labour. There had been nothing like it since the factory serfdom of a century before. At Monte Carlo the schedule went like this: 9 a.m., ballet class, then ballet rehearsal till mid-day; 2 p.m. to 4 p.m., ballet rehearsal again; 4 p.m. till 8.45 p.m., opera-ballet rehearsal; 9 p.m. special evening ballet performances at the Casino. Miss de Valois has told how, having had neither food nor drink since mid-day, she cried with fatigue as the wardrobe mistress bundled her into a butterfly costume for the evening show, *Carnaval*.

NINETTE DE VALOIS

She loved 'every minute' of the years she spent with Diaghilev, but the strain was too great—'one was invariably too worn out to feel really well'; and in any case she hankered after the opportunity to produce, to create, as well as to dance, in her own right. In later years she occasionally returned as guest dancer to the Diaghilev troupe; but her career was now a three-cornered affair very much after her heart's desire: Old Vic, Cambridge Festival Theatre, Abbey Theatre, Dublin. Some account has already been given of her Old Vic beginnings. At Cambridge she devised stylised movements for choruses in Greek plays and the like. In Dublin she produced and personally appeared in W. B. Yeats's plays for dancers. She led a hectic triangular life, and found it very heaven. Sadler's Wells, January, 1931, ended what may be termed the years of preparation. What followed is too famed to need detailing here.

Miss de Valois is small, neat, vital; works unconscionably hard. 'My main problem is how to cram thirty hours' work into twenty-four', is one of her sayings. Dancers watch her with wary affection. She knows how—and when—to be stern. One of the nicest things about her is her lucidity. *Invitation to the Ballet* is a model of polemics. For some people ballet is a world of languor, lilies, and woolly mysticism. For her it is one among various means of quenching man's saving appetite for beauty.

GRACIE FIELDS

To the pre-1939 generation, re-hearing the voice of Gracie—whose fame early outsoared her surname—is a wry as well as a joyous experience.

Each facet of that extraordinary voice, every swerve in those loyal Lancashire diphthongs, carries memories of the late 'twenties and mid-'thirties. Life then had a lingering bounty, and public perils were sometimes less menacing than they seemed. To present delights Miss Fields will thus add the luxury of wistful retrospect, always a pleasant mixture.

So much for what may be described as Gracie-plus. Gracie *qua* Gracie remains to be considered: a perplexing multiple phenomenon, as impossible to pin down as a bead of quicksilver. The versatility of her voice astounds. The entire register of music-hall stops is at her command. She gives us the sudden hoot, ladylike, unpremeditated and disconcerting. She is not afraid of frankly broad effects: roofless mouth and cold-in-the-nose are her occasional game.

Above all, she is adept at a peculiarly proletarian hoarseness which carries with it, perhaps, a touch of social portraiture: she can sing or shout with a larynx that is as though rusted by the humidity, heats, and chills of a thousand weaving and combing sheds among the hills and cobbles of her native North.

And yet, alongside all this, in uncanny duality, goes a pure and larklike warbling. If Gracie had been born in 1798 instead of 1898, she would have been captured young by some Italian singing master and turned into a coloratura sensation of the century. Bundled into crinolines for all rôles under the sun, classical and medieval included, she would have subjugated impossible arias by Rossini with roaring success at Drury Lane, the Haymarket, and Covent Garden, retiring in graceful old age with lace cap and the suffrages of Empire to a castle in Wales. The opportunities peculiar to our own time diverted her talents into more widely popular and homely channels. Nevertheless, opera was an early dream and one which has recurred from time to time.

During her clogs-and-shawl childhood at Rochdale, Lancs

GRACIE FIELDS

—school unwillingly in the morning, cotton mill more unwillingly still in the afternoon—she wanted to become a second Adelina Patti. After a taste of the music halls she decided to become a female George Formby instead. Twenty years or more later the long buried ambition stirred uneasily. She made a hobby of memorising Italian arias from the recordings of Galli-Curci and others. One night in revue at the Lyceum, heart in mouth, she sang a number from *La Traviata* at the request of Tetrazzini who sat back in her box and, so it is said, beamed encouragingly.

But, clearly, grand opera would have been far too solemn and rigid a medium for Gracie Fields, who, as a true child and practitioner of the halls, is licensed to laugh at most things, beginning with herself. She knows well how to bring a lump to the common throat, a tear to the general eye; but when the sentiment of sonny boy or white-haired granny is at its stickiest she is more likely than not to redeem the situation with that saving falsetto hoot. The voice suddenly flies to a remote upper storey where tear ducts are unknown and only the more antic spirits dwell. She is by no means the first player to trade in comic bathos, but few have done it with so nicely measured a touch. Gracie has said she could never be refined, however hard she tried. That, if she will pardon one for saying so, is nonsense. Refinement, in the sense of artistic means precisely adjusted to artistic ends, happens to be her strong point and stand-by.

Nobody can exactly define 'star quality'. It happens, inexplicably, irresistibly. Plenty can manage a short turn without losing favour. The owner of star quality can go on and on. He or she works into the public heart and there is no eviction, Gracie has star quality to her toes. But it is rooted, rooted in Rochdale and a hundred towns like it where, for anybody with half an eye, life is so rich in the player's raw material. The house at Capri came later in the routine of stardom: it never belonged. Molesworth Street is writ large across Gracie's burlesque. It was in Molesworth Street that she first met the char with ragged cap and other immortals of the revue sketches. The stage was an obvious predestination. Her mother laundered for the local theatre and always took her parcels round for delivery during full stage rehearsals. Gracie would go with her, stand in the wings and stare. The mimic faculty soon broke out of its shell: also the critical.

'What d'you think o' yon crowd?' she would be asked by her mother on their companionable homeward way from the theatre.

'Ah could lick th' lot.'

Soon she was singing at concerts in workingmen's clubs, a child marvel. School she hated, and dodged when she could. Gracie's own estimate is that she never had more than a year's effective teaching. Then started a queer double life, swinging between stage and cotton mill. For a month or two Gracie would tour with some juvenile troupe. At ten she got a £10 a week solo booking on a music hall circuit. At the end of tour or contract she usually had to go back to the spinning and winding frames for want of any other immediate job. There was no room for idle hands in Molesworth Street. Gracie must have undergone much pain of frustration at this time.

Success, when it did come, had the gradient of a rocket. In 1918 she and Archie Pitt, her first husband, started lucratively trudging the provinces with *Mr Tower of London*. When the news came one morning that the show had been booked for the Alhambra, thus receiving the revue's academic palm, Gracie, with sweet unreason, wept in the bedroom of a remote theatrical lodging. At sixteen she had paid her shilling into the Hippodrome gallery to see Violet Lorraine and Harry Tate in *Push and Go*. It was then that she resolved to break into the West End.

The way had been hard. After the Alhambra (1923) the way was broad, infernally busy and littered with contracts. She did all the inevitable things: sandwiched in a £100 a week solo act at the Coliseum, took on a business manager, picked, chose, turned down this offer, bargained about that. Money rolled in engulfingly. That rather frightened her at first.

Henceforth her life was unleisured and, in a sense, dedicated, not unlike that of royalty, as always happens to the

GRACIE FIELDS

Elect of the halls. But there was always time for something new and temerarious. For six months in 1928 she staggered the town and disappointed an envious minority by acting serenely well with Sir Gerald du Maurier in a play called *S.O.S.* at the St James's. It was a good part but brief and gave scope for other engagements. So Gracie also was singing twice nightly at the Coliseum and the Alhambra as well as in a Café Royal cabaret from midnight on—six shows a night.

Perhaps the tears shed in the provincial bedroom were not unreasonable after all. They may have been a shrewd prevision of the gilded treadmill: Palladium, Winter Garden, Coliseum and Alhambra again, Victoria Palace, Lyceum, Holborn Empire, New York's Palace Theatre, recordings, films, and all the rest of it—a triumphal and nerve-racking round.

By this time, of course, Gracie was a National Figure. A Freedom casket came from Rochdale (Molesworth Street was immensely proud), and, on the King's birthday in 1938, a C.B.E. When she had half a day to spare Gracie immersed herself in good works: her orphanage at Peacehaven means much to her.

There have been occasional shadows, among them ill-health, operating theatres, nursing homes. Her leaving for America, still a sick woman, in 1940, was widely regretted, but camp and factory concerts for troops on three Continents later brought renewed proof of the tumultuous affection in which she is held.

Gracie is now nearing her fiftieth year. The girl from Rochdale with the curiously Wagnerian chin, the hilarious, crowing laugh and the detached, quizzical regard has been one of the personalities of an epoch. One hears rumours of retirement. From memory and record she will never withdraw.

BACKROOM BOYS

LORD KEYNES

How to 'profile' Keynes, himself the arch-profilist, the man who has set down for ever the images of Clemenceau, Wilson, and Lloyd George, as they unwittingly sowed the dragon's teeth at Versailles? Especially did he catch the image of the aged Frenchman, who had 'one illusion—France, one disillusion—mankind, including Frenchmen and his colleagues not least'.

There he sat, the description continued, 'throned, in his grey gloves, on the brocade chair, dry in soul and empty of hope, very old and tired, but surveying the scene with a cynical and almost impish air'. The young man who saw and wrote this, concluded:

> These were the personalities of Paris—I forbear to mention other nations or lesser men: Clemenceau, aesthetically the noblest; the President, morally the most admirable; Lloyd George, intellectually the subtlest. Out of their disparities and weaknesses the Treaty was born, child of the least worthy attributes of each of its parents, without nobility, without morality, without intellect.

He left Paris where, at the age of thirty-six, he held (and gave up in despair) the post of the British Treasury's Principal Representative, and wrote one of the truly prophetic books of our time, *The Economic Consequences of the Peace*. He then continued to work for a world possessing those seemingly unattainable qualities of nobility, morality, and intellect.

John Maynard Keynes was essentially Cambridge. Among his many national tasks he found time to be High Steward of the City, in which he had been born fifty-nine years ago. His father, Registrary Emeritus of the University, is one of its senior citizens. His mother has been Mayor of the town. J. M. left Cambridge for Eton, but came back to King's, left King's for the Civil Service (India Office, 1906–08), but Cambridge snatched him from Whitehall and made him an economist with a Fellowship at King's. The only point where Cambridge seems to have been wrong is in listing him Twelfth Wrangler! The examiners must have been dazed. Twelfth Man, indeed! And what has become of the First Eleven?

Cambridge gave him up to the Treasury during the last war and afterwards, for part-time services, to Bloomsbury, where the range of his activities was astonishing. He was a busy journalist. As an economist he practised in the City as well as preaching in Cambridge, directed an investment trust, and an insurance company, and even did a little business as a theatrical agent (unpaid), arranging contracts for a Russian dancer, Lydia Lopokova, who was somewhat vague about her salary and what to do with it. Since she gave most of it away in tips, her budget was as deficient in balance as her dancing was perfect in that quality. One result of this highly specialised economic tuition which she received from Mr Keynes of King's was financial poise—another was a most happy marriage.

In the course of all he also did what most academic authorities on money do not: he became a rich man.

Keynes was the universal man, a specialised mathematician for whom the Lady Algebra is only a tenth Muse. He either practised or was patron of all the other gracious and learned arts and exercises. He was responsible for building a model theatre in Cambridge and giving it away: he made it a civic possession. His house in Gordon Square was the centre of a Bloomsbury galaxy, deriving largely from Cambridge, whose members included Virginia and L. S. Woolf, Clive and Vanessa Bell, Roger Fry and Duncan Grant, and an assorted Eminence of Stracheys—if one may coin a new noun of assembly for that formidable tribe. He collected, if he did not paint, the best pictures as well as the best company.

Meanwhile, Keynes continued the path of the heretic in economics—until finally orthodoxy claimed him for its own, as it has an odd way of treating the wiser innovators and the prescient rebels. He who had bitterly criticised the Return to Gold as an aggravation of the Great Depression was made a Director of the Bank of England and sat in the temple whose priests he had scourged.

In 1931 he had suggested that 'the bankers of the world are bent on suicide', and he had also described this class 'as the most romantic and least realistic of men'. He had also warned the 'friends of gold' that they would have to be 'extremely wise and moderate if they are to avoid a Revolution' (this in September, 1930).

His campaign against worship of the Gold Standard and against Deflation was justified by the facts. When the war, consequent on that Nazi Revolution which we did not avoid, broke out, he advocated compulsory savings, a scheme which has in part been adopted. His directness of mind and simplicity of prose made him Whitehall's model of exposition. The Chancellor was indeed lucky in his background. The scene of our mammoth war-finance was not only a Kingsley Wood: it was a plantation of Keynes. The name, incidentally, is Norman (very right for the Bank of England) being anglicised *chênes*. Hearts of oak, but not heads of oak, are our Keynes.

Could a man be busier? Hardly. Yet he was Chairman of C.E.M.A. and of its advisory panels which planned the development of music, painting, drama and ballet as elements of popular culture, 'joys in widest commonalty spread'. Under his rule C.E.M.A. was honoured with permanent status and a royal charter. So Keynes was the first Chairman and main architect of the Arts Council of Great Britain. It is no flattery to say of Lord Keynes that he was the most multifarious of specialists. He had as gentle a voice as ever said 'no' to nonsense and as kind an eye as ever scrutinised a minute or a set of accounts and immediately saw the mistake. A ballet or a balance sheet? He was the acute judge of either.

Americans call patrons of the arts 'angels'. He was the least ineffectual of that celestial kind. A Highbrow? Say, rather, in a word of Mrs Browning's, a Muse-Brow. But no austere one.

He was intensely interested in the future of the Crystal Palace as a home of all popular pleasures. He once wrote in a charming essay on a now forgotten Prime Minister:

> Mr Bonar Law's inordinate respect for Success is noteworthy. He is capable of respecting even an intellectualist who turns our right.

We can honestly turn the phrase on the author. He did get things right. Be the values musical or financial, he knew all the answers. He has destroyed the definition of an Economist as a man who is always dull and always wrong. With Lord Keynes at the desk, or on the dais, what was once the Dismal Science managed both to be scientific and exciting, as lively as Mozart, indeed quite a gay young party—just down from Cambridge.

SIR JOHN ANDERSON

THE Right Honourable Sir John Anderson, P.C., G.C.B., G.C.S.I., G.C.I.E., lately Chancellor of the Exchequer; Lord President of the Council; Home Secretary and Minister of Home Security; Lord Privy Seal; Governor of Bengal; Under-Secretary of State, Home Office; Under-Secretary to the Lord Lieutenant of Ireland; Chairman of the Board of Inland Revenue; Secretary, Ministry of Shipping; Secretary to the Insurance Commissioners.... The sonorous roll of honours and titles fits the man. Wherever Sir John makes his stately progress the fanfare of heralds is faintly audible: *incessu patuit aliquis*.

At an early age he and Destiny agreed that he should become a Great Man, and these two equals have kept each other to the bargain. In the lexicon of that bright youth there was no such word as failure, and the man has had no public occasion since to look it up. Perhaps he came nearest to it at the Home Office in handling enemy aliens.

Of scientific mind, with Scottish thoroughness he takes all knowledge for his province, and Ministers, officials, and deputations have more than once been dumbfounded by the range and precision of what he knows and by the timeliness and obedience of his memory. So generous is he of information, so anxious that no one in future shall have excuse for ignorance, that his speeches are apt to turn into lectures. He is not an artist: he cannot select and omit. It is said that once, after he had given an explanation to Parliament of earth waves set up by bomb explosions near structures, the House adjourned unexpectedly early 'suffering from monolithic concussion'.

His knowledge is supported by a gubernatorial manner; he sits his seat, like a Lord Chief Justice, heavily and firmly, and always seems a little larger than life. One of his colleagues described him as presiding over a committee of Ministers 'with the impressive wisdom and tolerance of the family solicitor who is also a Presbyterian elder and a senior uncle'. In his maiden speech to the Commons he quoted Browning, no doubt a reminiscence of his Edinburgh youth.

To this manner is added a wide experience of administration—

SIR JOHN ANDERSON

a decision is a necessity of his diet. Sir John likes to see a move, even if it is only to the next step, for he retains his native caution and distrusts the short cut. He reads his papers, and thus acquires a high grade in the secret Order of Merit which officials confer upon their political chiefs. He does more: he understands them better than their authors, and can remember them and make use of them. He will work at almost anything, and is very nearly imperturbable in action. He backs his people, and has great personal bravery, as Ireland and Bengal can testify. It is not surprising that Mr Churchill, with affection and appositeness, called him his 'old war horse'.

In the running of the war he played an unobtrusive but vital part: the reconciliation of differences until a policy emerged, the formulation of the facts, the examination of machinery, a very present help in inter-Departmental trouble. In some ways he is more practical than Lord Milner, but with less passion or boldness or sense of urgency. In Parliament he has been much more of a success than could have been expected of a Civil Servant, but it cannot be said that the House has really taken him to its bosom; that would imply an indelicate familiarity with a person of natural pomp and circumstance. He is respected, and because he knows his stuff he is listened to, sometimes for quite a long time.

With all these gifts of mind and character what does he lack that he is not absolutely pre-eminent? Not warmth in personal relations, for those who know him best can often feel a glow as from a Raeburn portrait. A gift for intimacy, perhaps; long years of high office, begun as a serious young man, have put a stiff resplendent uniform upon him in which he bends with difficulty. Perhaps some diffidence about himself—not about his powers, but about his own personality; his outward assurance covers a shy man who fears to let himself go. A distrust of enthusiasm, which seems to him undisciplined and illogical; a failure to understand the very ordinary man, who is a man 'for a' that'. When he drinks the toast of the Immortal Memory what does he really think of Burns? Does he prefer Browning?

Legends and stories are gathering around Sir John; he is on

the way to becoming a National Monument, and that does not happen, in his lifetime, to a small man. A popular figure in the ordinary sense he is not, neither on the platform nor on the radio. In earlier days Whitehall intimates called him 'Jonathan', but the crowd will never stop his car and call him 'Good old Johnny'. His gravity is not a cloak for mental deficiencies; it is the warp and woof of his mind. He is neither romantic nor magnetic; he is a great, an invaluable, administrator.

SIR WILFRID EADY

ON his official duties the Civil Servant takes a triple vow of Obedience, Anonymity and Silence. The Rule is salutary. On public obedience to whatever Government is in power rests the whole tradition of the Service, the unique contribution to the principles of public administration that this country has given. Less than anonymity would be, in the long run, unjust to the intricate hierarchy which is the peculiar structure of the British Civil Service. Silence is necessary because public disagreement with the policy of the Government would be intolerable, and public agreement obsequious.

Nor is there any reason to believe that the public would have it otherwise. The public servants must remain unseen, unheard, shadowy figures in the background. Deprived of the experience of the market-place which alone brings out manliness, secure in their office, these cautious persons pursue their unexciting lives in mediocre surroundings; such was a description of the public service in the House of Lords.

Occasionally the chances of duty bring a name to popular notice, and the owner of it is exposed to publicity which is doubtless unwelcome. This has happened to Sir Wilfrid Eady more than once, and not always fortunately. It is certainly rare for a Civil Servant to find himself engaged in a task which arouses continuous interest among very large sections of the public, and contains within itself the sudden reversals of fortune which make drama and 'news'.

This happened in the negotiations with the Argentine Government. It seemed that our meat supplies were at stake, and everybody was interested in that. The value of the British-owned railways in the Argentine, that great contribution to the development of the country, was clearly sinking and might disappear; there were many thousands of families concerned, for in the past their modest investments had produced a necessary part of their income. There was finally the question of the sterling balances, an esoteric subject but of crucial importance to a small number of informed persons.

The drama came from the conduct of the negotiations, with

the familiar words of 'crisis', 'breakdown', and finally and suddenly, agreement. In all this there was news value; there was even novelty in the fact of ultimate and precise agreement on matters of sharp controversy and political feeling between two independent countries. This aroused curiosity on the personality of the official to whom the Government had given the responsibility for leading the negotiations.

Sir Wilfrid Eady was born in the Argentine, the son of one of the young engineers who helped to build the railways. His birthplace was the small and ancient village of Villa Nueva, where, during his recent visit, he was made an Honorary Neighbour by special Municipal Decree, and, at the request of the Committee of Citizens, presented a flagpole to commemorate the occasion. Nearly fifty years ago he returned to England, and was educated at Clifton, where he enjoyed long-distance running and fought in the finals of the Public Schools Boxing Championship, an early training which probably helped him in the negotiations, and, reading Classics, at Jesus College, Cambridge, of which he is an Honorary Fellow.

Then the Civil Service by Open Examination, and an unusual variety of official experience, including nearly twenty years in the Ministry of Labour, a large share in the creation of the Unemployment Assistance Board, the organisation of A.R.P., the introduction of the Purchase Tax at the Board of Customs, and finally transfer to the Treasury in nominal charge of Finance. Nominal because he worked as close colleague and pupil of Lord Keynes, of whom he cannot speak with restraint. It is related that Lord Keynes said to him, 'If I had had you young enough, I could, with patience, have taught you the elements of modern economic thought. As it is, I must remain content to believe that you understand the art of administration.' He accompanied Lord Keynes to Bretton Woods. Earlier he negotiated the Canadian Loan agreement. It may well be inferred that during the three months in Buenos Aires Sir Wilfrid Eady had to draw upon all he had learned in differing schools.

The execution of tasks so varied, so complex and concrete, has made Sir Wilfrid one of the best known of our central administrators. His mind is one of the swiftest, and so is his pen, his grasp of essentials immediate, and his sense of the ridiculous, which sometimes has got him into trouble, has on balance been a valuable asset to the negotiator. He takes pride in his profession of Public Administration, and believes in 'that universal solvent, the wild living intellect of man'. He has few prejudices, and keeps his principles to himself. Throughout his service to the State he has retained the affection of his colleagues and his many friends, and their admiration of his gifts.

He finds relief from Whitehall in an unaffected home circle, where his own intelligence is matched by that of his family, in amateur play-writing, and in a wide-ranging love of books. He is something of a scholar in literature, but thinks, like Dr Johnson, that a bad book is better than no book at all, and has an unashamed liking for crime stories because only there is it certain that law and order will triumph in the end.

In the final analysis he appears to enjoy nearly everything that comes along. Indeed it is possible to suspect that he really enjoyed himself in Buenos Aires. At fifty-six, fresh from his Argentine exploits, he is unspoiled by success. It is men like Sir Wilfrid Eady, uniting ability, integrity and good humour to the vows of Obedience, Anonymity and Silence, who are the hidden glory of their time, and it is they who have made the British Civil Service 'the finest in the world'.

LORD BEVERIDGE

THE overwhelming fact about Lord Beveridge is that he is a man of action. Life is to him a series of campaigns against inefficiency and injustice. If he strikes an unfamiliar note in Whitehall, it is far more because he is the great captain who has left his troops, the administrator without a department, rather than the scholar who has wandered from his study. He *is* a great scholar. But knowledge to him is a means, not an end.

He lives in the future; he has always done so. Yesterday is only of interest to him as a guide to tomorrow. He never talks about his own past achievements, not out of any false modesty but simply because it seems irrelevant to him.

When you see this white-haired, rosy-cheeked, vigorous sexagenarian dodging in and out of taxis, or bounding, rucksack on shoulder, up the steps of the Reform Club, it does not occur to you to wonder what Sir William was like as a young man, nor to think of him as a Scotsman born in India, the son of a Judge. His activities compel too much attention for one to look back. When you see him in his real element—presiding at an inquiry with Service high-ups or fuel magnates or famous social reformers appearing to give evidence—even a lifelong friend does not find leisure to recall the days of 1909–11 when Mr Churchill, as Home Secretary, brought in 'the boy Beveridge' at the request of the Sidney Webbs to start the Labour Exchanges and get unemployment insurance going.

Again, his plan for fuel rationing during the war aroused much controversy, but neither its author nor anyone else was particularly concerned to compare it with his successful plan for food rationing in the last war. In the academic field he was Director of the London School of Economics from 1919 to 1937, and he created 'the School' as we know it today. But with his achievements there completed, he fulfilled his rôle as Master of University College, Oxford, without reference to them as precedents.

But from this buoyant freshness, do not infer volatility or lack of persistent personality. Nothing could be further from the truth. Always, ineluctably and irreducibly, he has been and is

LORD BEVERIDGE

his distinctive self. If he is asked to do a job he does it in his own way—and he gets it done! If its final consummation depends on the decision of a Government, as with fuel rationing, there may be delay, debate, negation. But there is an unwritten rule, first established in 1909, that a Beveridge plan *always* goes through. If it is some time before he finds favour again with a Government, he shrugs his shoulders and pushes ahead with some other job, which may already have been commissioned by the self-same Government.

One cannot help comparing him with that other great contemporary figure in the sphere of economics, theoretical and applied, Lord Keynes. Whereas Keynes was the deductive economist, starting always from first principles, Beveridge works inductively. For instance, he becomes the social investigator, probing poverty from Toynbee Hall in the slums of East London; then writes a book—*Unemployment: A Problem of Industry*; then invents the Labour Exchanges and the administration of unemployment insurance.

His features fit his faculties. The erect, longbacked head tells you of his power of assimilation. The broad fine forehead explains his ability for impromptu 'dictation'—an art somewhere between literature and oratory, in which it is difficult to believe that even Mr Churchill is his superior. The grey eyes and fighter's chin give you the born leader, to whom the opportunity of taking big decisions on his own initiative is the breath of life. If you had to name his weakness there is little doubt what an admirer would choose: he is and has always been constitutionally incapable of concealing his opinion of people he is working with. He lacks that particular form of cunning which is the stock-in-trade of the small-town politician.

'Outside the office' he is the softest-hearted, the gayest of men. But work has always been sacred, and those whose neglect or relative slowness hold up his dynamic progress pay a penalty which leaves on many weaker vessels a permanent scar.

When, in the middle of war, Mr Bevin appointed him Chairman of the Committee on Skilled Men in the Services, and Mr Greenwood at the same time asked him to undertake an inter-departmental inquiry into social insurance and other allied services, neither appointment at that moment seemed particularly glamorous. To the average pundit who had passed sixty it would have looked as though the end had come; instead of that 'Beveridge' stepped on to a new plane in our national life and revealed the plenitude of his powers at the moment when the nation most needed them.

SIR JOHN BOYD ORR

For over two hundred years Aberdeen has been the nurse of dieticians. The first wave of nutritional fervour that swept through the medical profession was started by George Cheyne, a twenty-stone general practitioner from Aberdeenshire, who became a fashionable London physician in the days of good Queen Anne. Aberdonians have been discernible in the several tides of enthusiasm since Cheyne's day, and on the crest of the last, riding it like a whirlwind, has been Sir John Boyd Orr, Director of the Rowett Institute at Aberdeen and head of the North of Scotland College of Agriculture.

More than twenty-five years ago Orr came to Aberdeen, unknown save for a little book on the Scottish Free Churches dispute of 1904. That book was enough to give him the reputation of a Covenanter, but perhaps people did not appreciate its significance. For the county of Ayr, in which Orr was born and bred, is still steeped in the lore of the Killing Time, and Orr with his long nose, long jaw, long head, and long tongue would have qualified on sight to be the central figure at a conventicle or a leader of proletarians at Drumclog or Bothwell Brig. In fact, since he went to Aberdeen, he has turned Scotland into a battlefield of sorts, in which his enemies have been Poverty, Want, and Disease.

He entered the conflict uncommonly well equipped. He is a Master of Arts, a Doctor of Medicine, and a Doctor of Science of Glasgow University. In the first German War he collected a D.S.O., an M.C., and a mention. In later years he has become an LL.D., an F.R.S., a J.P., and a Knight Bachelor. When he went to the Rowett Institute it was an unpretentious affair in a corner of the College of Agriculture, intended for quiet study of the problems of animal nutrition. But rickets in pigs and deficiency disorders in sheep could not retain Orr's attention long. Human beings suffer from rickets and under-nourishment as well as animals, and the diseases of malnutrition are not bounded by the shores of Great Britain.

And so, from a back room, the Rowett Institute has expanded into a sizeable village, a long line of perhaps characteristically incongruous buildings. The farm offices, on something like the Dutch model, are capped by two towering silos. The flat rectangle of the administrative block contains the laboratories, while the Reid Library and the Strathcona Hall cater for the intellectual and social leisure of the inmates. Crofts and farms have been added to the operational surroundings, and the Institute's last and greatest acquisition was signalised in a merger with the North of Scotland College of Agriculture, in which the principalship of the College and the Chair of Agriculture fell to the Director, and the management of the College farms to the Farm Manager, of the Institute.

Nor has Orr confined the expansion of the Institute to its purely physical development. It embodies the headquarters of the Imperial Bureau of Animal Nutrition, and is the fountain whence issues—or did until the war—a steady stream of papers dedicated to the exposition of the subject of Dietetics in all its aspects real and imaginary.

Gradually the energy of the Director concentrated upon investigating the problems of human nutrition. It has been said that Orr has a long tongue. He likes to talk—no unusual attribute; but people, having heard him talk, like him to go on talking, rather a deviation from common practice. He could, as the Scotch saying has it, 'talk the hin' leg aff a cuddy'. His is a magnificent bedside manner lost to Harley Street, a compelling pow lost to the pulpit. In the art of bringing an audience round he has few equals.

His thesis of Peace through Plenty is easier to criticise than to analyse. Modern science is much more fluid in its tenets than the public realises, and the fluctuations in expert opinion upon food and nutrition are wide and frequent. In the main, however, Orr has stuck to his contention that diet and income must be considered together. Before the war he maintained that 'a diet completely adequate for health, according to modern standards, is reached at an income level above that of 50 per cent of the population'. He found that 'the average diet' of the poorest four and a half millions of the population was 'deficient in every constituent'. He concluded that 'as income increases, disease and death-rate decrease'. Therefore, the dietary of the poorest must be improved.

When it was decided that the United Nations should devise a common policy for the control of their food production and distribution, Orr was an inevitable choice as a British delegate. He was, however, more than a delegate at Hot Springs. He identified himself with the projects there decided to such an extent that when the conference was over, he personified the conference. The months since Hot Springs have lengthened into years, but he of all who attended still believes passionately in it and in its practicability.

For a man in his sixties Orr has retained a remarkable youthfulness of mind. Its quality is not merely that of vigour but of boyish pleasure in being able to champion a cause. His passion for the milky way in nutrition has some characteristics of the nebulae in it, and there is some ground for the criticism that his best laid schemes have never come near enough to actuality to prove that they will not 'gang agley'. Yet there has never been a reformer who could make his reforms so palatable to the public, and seldom an enthusiast who could come down to earth so naturally.

DR CHARLES HILL

DR HILL is the Secretary of the British Medical Association, and the leader in its fight against a salaried State medical service. He is also the Radio Doctor, the gruff, genial, gusty expounder of physical intimacies, the man with a 'mikeside' manner (proletarian). Anyone who expected a Radio Doctor to be a glib son of Galen, just a vocal replica of a B.B.C. voice, trailing a cloud of medical letters after his name, has been disappointed. All who wanted heart-to-heart, or even bowel-to-bowel, talks, spoken in the idiom and the accent of the people, have had them.

Born some forty years ago in North London, the youngest of three children, Charles Hill was left fatherless when still an infant. His mother had a hard struggle to bring up her family, and her hands must have been full when the infant Charles began to walk. One suspects that he got out of the toddling stage at a record speed, and that he did not linger at the bottom of the class in the elementary school which started him off on a successful career. An unbroken succession of scholarships carried him to St Olave's School in South-East London, and from there to Trinity, Cambridge. He took his B.A. with a first in Part I. of the Natural Science Tripos, and ended up with a Cambridge M.D. some years after leaving the London Hospital.

When Hill was a student at the London, and later a 'house' doctor, he kept himself by lecturing on biology in the London University Extension Scheme and for the W.E.A. He 'won through' in medicine in the hard way, and all the time knew that the next step depended on his own efforts. He certainly could not afford the familiar failure in one or two examinations that the average student accepts as part and parcel of the general 'cussedness' of medical examiners.

Hill now occupies two positions, one official and the other unofficial, which are somewhat paradoxical for a man of his training. After a brief period as a medical officer in a mental hospital and two years as Deputy Medical Officer of Health for Oxford, he was appointed Assistant Secretary of the B.M.A. in 1932, and is now Secretary of this body.

DR CHARLES HILL

With a relatively brief experience of clinical medicine he yet occupies the key position in an organisation the great majority of whose members are general practitioners. He is thus at the hub of medical affairs at a time which all doctors regard as epochal in the history of medicine, at a time when the profession is simultaneously subjected to the severe internal strains imposed by the war and to the external stress of governmental demand for reform. It is the kind of challenge to action that Hill likes, and his response to it has gained the full confidence of the 48,000 men and women who belong to the B.M.A.

While his experience of administration would obviously fit a man for much of the kind of work expected of the secretary of the B.M.A., few would have guessed that the same experience and the same man would create the Radio Doctor, who, like Tommy Handley, is as popular with the intellectual as he is with the broad middle classes.

'Fancy the secretary of the B.M.A. telling you to go 'ome with fish and chips under yer arm', as one bus companion was heard to say to another. Hill's first broadcast nine years ago was on the report of the B.M.A. Nutrition Committee, and for three years he arrived at Broadcasting House at eight o'clock every Wednesday morning to talk on the *Kitchen Front*. He has broadcast on the schools programme, has given talks on simple physiology, and on ordinary medical subjects under the heading of *What is it?* In fact, he is continuing his lectures on biology.

What is the secret of his success? It is doubtful whether this can be traced to a wide interest in health matters on the part of the public. A highly developed—some have said over-developed —broadcasting technique is not the answer. Much of the attraction lies in the fact that Hill talks to the man in the street in his own lingo. He is content to drive home one point in one talk, with verbal agility, humour—simile: 'that black-coated worker, the prune'.

But this does not explain his appeal to the intellectual. He appeals to the intellectual for the same reason that Joad appeals to the low-brow: he is a first-class entertainer and is never dull.

OBSERVER PROFILES

And he captivates all 'brows' because his approach is so unlike that of a professional man. He does not hesitate. He does not qualify his statements with 'in my opinion', or 'I am inclined to believe'. He is utterly uncautious but never inaccurate. Any fellow doctor wanting to criticise his broadcasting would lose sight of the fact that this quite unexpectedly booming voice over the wireless is doing a first-class job in preventive medicine.

The man himself is in appearance the very opposite of the popular conception of the doctor, the doctor of Frith's picture in the Tate Gallery. If George Robey had not filled the part of Sancho Panza, the Radio Doctor could easily have been coached into a passable understudy. Hill would not tilt at windmills, or lead a crusade.

Although he has a fine academic record he has not got an academic mind, nor has he much taste for the leisured pursuits of the cultured. Nobody could be less the dilettante. He is an aggressive and practical thinker, a doughty opponent in argument—able to use the rapier as well as the bludgeon—quick to spot the chinks in the other man's armour. He has an almost uncanny power over men in committee and almost too easily dominates others.

As a speaker he can on occasion rise to oratorical heights. He has force and is a man of strong ambitions. His power to persuade, to lead, to think on his feet accurately and rapidly, his shrewd assessment of men and movements, ought to take him on to the floor of the House of Commons. Whether or not his public ambition lies there, his private life hinges round his home and his wife and four children, who manage him as easily and skilfully as he manages others.

MINDS

BERNARD SHAW

GEORGE BERNARD SHAW moves on towards his century. For a new postscript to *Back to Methuselah*, recently promoted by the Oxford University Press to be a World's Classic, he wrote:

> Though I am very far from being as clever and well-informed as people think, I am not below the average in political capacity: yet in my eighty-ninth year I am no more fit to rule millions of men than is a boy of twelve.
>
> Physically I am failing: my senses, my locomotive powers, my memory are decaying at a rate which threatens to make a Struldbrug of me if I persist in living: yet my mind still feels capable of growth, for my curiosity is keener than ever. My soul goes marching on: and, if the Life Force would give me a body as durable as my mind, and I knew better how to feed and lodge and dress and behave, I might begin a political career as a junior civil servant and evolve into a capable Cabinet Minister in another hundred years or so.

There speaks the practical Methuselist, the dramatist-philosopher whose life-work culminated, a quarter of a century ago, in the least tractable, least actable, largest, deepest, longest of his plays, which needs nearly a week of evenings to perform, the Metabiological Pentateuch whose message was this. Man dies when still a child. Let him abandon such folly. Let him live and live and learn and learn. Let him turn to Methuselah, as well as to the ant, and be wise. Creative evolution is a matter of resolve, not of destiny. Will to live and live you will. Man is at present only reaching his poor, few years of indiscretion; he must now achieve his whole centuries of discretion. Only so can the world be saved.

OBSERVER PROFILES

Unique among preachers, Shaw has lived his own sermon. Almost a Crimean War baby, he has endured into the age of atomic warfare—and is still in fettle to give overweening Science the scolding it deserves. Hail—and not for years farewell—Methuselah!

There is longevity in his breed, which may have been a help. His grandmother, after producing fifteen children in twenty-two years, lived to be eighty-eight. His ancestry is a tough one, including Oliver Cromwell and Macduff. Who would have thought the old man had so much (regicide) blood in him? The Shaws or Sheachs were septs of the Macduffs: later, like many other Scots, they revenged the early colonisation of Scotland by the Irish. One went with King Billy to the Boyne and earned thereby the victor's reward of land in Cork and Kilkenny. The Shaws became a large 'Ascendancy' clan and held the usual posts and offices. The family drifted a little downward and George Carr Shaw, Bernard's father, hardly kept the old Shaw standard. He was a failure in business and a sleepy, collapsible drinker who became impossible in company but never maltreated his children.

The young Bernard went to the Wesleyan Connectional School in Dublin, but looked after his own education. He obstinately refused to earn a living in commerce, came to London with his mother, and set up professionally as an unsuccessful novelist. Meanwhile he realised that London, with its libraries, galleries, museums, theatres, concert halls, Fabian Society, platform rhetoricians, and myriad specimens of *homo insipiens*, far outstripped Oxford as a University for observant youth. Avoiding the collegiate stamp and the educational routine, and so escaping from all tutorial malformation, he set out to become the best informed man of his time and triumphantly did so. In the course of this self-selected schooling he also picked up the clearest and most vigorous prose-style in all the various histories of English pamphleteering, soap-box oratory, formal lecturing, musical and dramatic criticism, and epistolary technique. His career, whether the pedagogues like it or not, is a cogent and lasting incitement to dodging their attentions.

BERNARD SHAW

As a Fabian Socialist, he learned much from the Webbs, Graham Wallas, Sidney Olivier, and the other sages of the new Collectivism. But he was never absorbed into the Positivist universe, fashionable with the late Victorian intellectuals. Indeed he prefers mysticism to materialism and sees no point in evicting God from the popular temples in order to instal the General Medical Council. Butler's criticism of Darwinian determinism made a powerful impact on his mind and developed his belief in a Creative Evolution, in whose grip he believes that he is working. What is the end of the cosmic process? Not one easily appreciated by the Average Sensual Man. Shaw's Lilith prophesies that 'after passing a million goals they (Man and Woman) press on to the goal of redemption from the flesh, to the vortex freed from matter, to the whirlpool in pure intelligence that when the world began was a whirlpool in pure force'.

Yet Shaw is no complete ascetic. To his awareness of sensuous beauty his writings on painting and music are eloquent testimony. He can consider a nut cutlet as others a mutton one. Neither carnivore nor Bacchanalian, he has enjoyed all the energy of both without the aid of gore or grape. Mrs Patrick Campbell said that it was just as well: 'Give him a steak and no woman in London would be safe.' In order to silence Frank Harris's nonsense on the subject Shaw has made public his own *vie amoureuse*. It began, physically, at twenty-eight and seems to have been very largely thereafter a correspondence course. In his wildly productive period (the 'nineties) he poured out letters to Ellen Terry, whom he worshipped without meeting, and to Florence Farr, Mrs Patrick Campbell, and Janet Achurch as well. Never in its history can the British Post Office have conveyed daily and unwittingly so much admirable prose in penny packets. Did A. B. Walkley, critic, Civil Servant (P.O.) (Trotter of *Fanny's First Play* and dedicatee of *Man and Superman*) comprehend what his foot-slogging minions were continually collecting and bearing to all the beauties of the town?

It wore G. B. S. down, inevitably. He has observed that

every really busy man should take a year's holiday at forty to recover physique and poise of mind. Shaw for once failed to take his own advice. 'If I make another stroke with a pen', he wrote to Ellen Terry, 'I shall go mad. Oh, Ellen, I am the world's pack-horse and it beats my ribs unmercifully.' At forty-two he collapsed and was rescued by an Irish lady of property, Charlotte Payne-Townshend, who took him to the high Surrey heaths, cured him, married him, and was his perfect wife and warden for the rest of her long life. As Shaw became less of the rubious-bearded rebel and more of the Public Institution, reporter-hunted, bore-pursued, the partnership must have been hard work at times. But Mrs Shaw had married when too old to bear a first child. This gave her time and strength for supervision of that Lion's Den which the top-floor perch in Adelphi Terrace was soon to be.

Shaw has become the greatest theatrical figure of the day while hating and despising what most people mean by theatre. His loves, outside the home, have been as various as numerous, Ellen Terry and Alphabetical Reform, 'Mrs Pat' and a green diet, Duse and the Sidney Webbs, Ibsen and Wagner, Municipal Socialism and Creative Evolution. His hates are for all things cruel, stupid, and pompous, especially for all things pretentious, whether sacerdotal or scientific. Flamboyance he fled from: see his criticisms of Irving and Bernhardt. At present, over ninety years old, and by no means so physically diminished as he sometimes claims, he is the nearest thing that lives among us to a 'whirlpool of pure intelligence'. But the mental vortex is not all. Shaw has not forgotten, in the ninety odd years of his nonage, the pleasures of kindness as well of paradox and of mischief. He has stood on his head in public and emptied his pockets in private. To the 'nineties he was a clown, to us he is a World's Classic. He was Joey to Mrs Pat and, when she died, she babbled of him so. Not for her to understand Methuselah, purposing and achieving the conquest of the flesh and the triumph of the mind. But such is he, our major prophet of the Life Force and, what is more, so aboundingly its vessel.

H. G. WELLS

At a time when Science has afflicted the world in horrible fact with what once seemed to be the fantasies of the prophetic mind, it is well to remember that young man who looked so astonishingly far ahead. H. G. Wells did not only foresee the scientific menace that now pours robot comets into the air and bodes further rocketings; he outlined also the political preventives.

He was not in his element as the organiser of campaigns, or as the sedulous ant of committee-work; he was the large-scale cartographer of human liberation from drudgery and destruction, drawing the map of a World Order rapidly, repeatedly, variously. He began his literary career with his fascinating scientific romances, hurling men into lunar spaces or making them grow giant-wise on the food of the gods; he then tried to rescue them from lunacy and to fit them for being human. He brought plans, federations, Utopias descending helpfully on the obstinate skull of *homo insipiens*. His victims enjoyed the services and paid for them, only reserving the right to remain as strictly insipient as before.

It would be totally unjust to regard Wells as a Utopian dreamer only: he was essentially the practical prophet. For example, if the British War Office had paid the slightest attention to the observations made just at the close of the Boer War, by an ex-shop-assistant turned science-master and Socialist pamphleteer, the war of 1914 might have been won in a quarter of the time. To read now Wells's *Anticipations* is to be astounded by his range of warning and prevision. In 1902 he told the cavalry men that in any great war there would be a deadlock of defensive marksmen; to break this he envisaged land-cruisers or tanks. In 1902, seven years before the flimsiest aeroplane had crossed the Channel, he was writing:

> By day the victor's aeroplanes will sweep down upon the apparatus of all sorts in the adversary's rear, and will drop explosives and incendiary matters upon them, so that no apparatus or camp shelter will any longer be safe. At night

his high floating searchlights will go to and fro and discover and check every desperate attempt to relieve or feed the exhausted marksmen of the fighting line. . . . A general advance will occur under the aerial van, ironclad road fighting machines may perhaps play a considerable part in this, and the enemy's line of marksmen will be driven back or starved into surrender, or broken up and hunted down.

It was uncanny prescience.

He outlined, also in 1902, the rise of the highly organised State and the advantage with which a totalitarian nation would start a war.

The State that has not incorporated with its fighting organisation all its able-bodied manhood and all its material substance, its roads, vehicles, engines, foundries, and all its resources of food and clothing; the State which at the outbreak of war has to bargain with railway and shipping companies, replace experienced station-masters by inexperienced officers, and haggle against alien interests for every sort of supply, will be at an overwhelming disadvantage against a State which has . . . organised every element in its being.

Wells the prophet developed later into Wells the historian. But his intuitive grip on the shape of things to come was even firmer than his instructed hold upon the outline of things past.

Though having a mercurial vitality and quenchless curiosity, not commonly connected with the Englishman, Wells was none the less pure native. He was a Kentishman as well as a cosmopolite. What more English than his origin (his father was a professional cricketer mentioned in Wisden for a feat of bowling)? What more English than the descriptions of Kentish country and character in *Kipps* and *Mr Polly*? He had the cherry-ripe look of his shire and his moods could be tart or sweet as a pippin. He never wrote with affection of the sombre landscapes: he liked Riviera sunshine in his later years, but London and the

Home Counties held most of his life. Here he would make his home and invent odd games, talk and enchant and quarrel and decant the generous vintage of a bubbling mind. He was ever a quick mover from idea to idea and he compounded a hundred pills to purge the distempers of mankind. He was, in his expository way, the Master Alchemist, the prime dispenser of salves for society. But how he could, in *Tono Bungay*, satirise the minor and commercial alchemy!

Like nearly all Socialists, Wells was a vigorous individualist. He preached co-operation with more fervour than he practised it. He was, in any argument or campaign, a fiery particle. Few men have brought more warmth of passion to the advocacy of cool, rational ways. Above all he hated all mystical hocus-pocus, all bans and vetoes, all obscurantism. Free inquiry was the breath of life to him; hence his furious conflicts with the Roman Catholic Church. He had a bout of theism at one time. But his God was very Wellsian, rather the benign invisible King of a World-State than any conventional President of the Immortals.

Wells went about anticipating everybody and everything. Tanks, aeroplanes, the war in the air, on the one hand: the cartoonists' Little Man, e.g., Kipps and Polly, on the other. Scratch an Englishman and you find a Protestant: but not a glum one. There is always something to be found there of the laughing cavalier as well as of the serious roundhead. Wells was a chuckling, as well as a combative, man: his novels were full of laughter and his argument had the bite of a happily pugnacious man. He continually piped us to the feast of reason, bringing to it his own condiments, his zest for all things liberal, the Attic salt of his wit, and, above all, the red pepper which so abundantly flavoured his anger against muddle and misrule.

GILBERT MURRAY

GILBERT MURRAY, another of our active octogenarians, now looks out on a world containing far less of the classical education which he has so brilliantly, even so passionately, served. The 'grand old fortifying curriculum' has very largely lost its status, its followers, and its utility as a gateway to professions. There were many reasons for that: pupils of other inclination and with no classical aptitude were too often subpoena'd for attendance in ancient courts where Demosthenes and Cicero droned on to vex the dull ears of a drowsy class. Too often, also, the classics were projected at young heads without tutorial sympathy and without any humour or humanity on the dais. None strove harder than Murray to rescue Greece and its glories from such injustice and such persecution. At the sound of his high, exciting speech in the lecture-room (his eyes would flash and his voice seemed to quiver at the beauty of the words he taught and quoted) or beneath the persuasion of his translator's pen, turning the dusty answer of the crib into leaping Swinburnian lines, the classics were no longer an affliction of task-work. They were a window on the world.

For any pupil wearied by the dull orthodoxy of a Greek-and-Latin routine to read Murray's *History of Greek Literature* (mainly written before he was thirty) was to find old, baffling, and even boring texts turned into illumined missals. One was taken behind the grammar and the scansion to the men and women, the ardours and endurances of ancient Greece. Their history was linked with ours. Their drama, its beauties mingled with strange, cruel, incredible saga-plots, had been so foolishly taught by many just as exam-fodder, without background, and with no relation to the ancient myths and the high, bright landscape of their background. Murray, who could so vividly imagine the far-off stage among the marbled avenues or the olivery-silvery mountains, gave new meaning to old tasks.

Some said that his translations of the austere Greek belied the spareness of the original, that a simple *oimoi* ('alas') would become 'Oh the pain, oh the pain over Ilium breaking' or words to that richer effect. Perhaps the criticism of superfluency in phrase and of a certain over-eagerness for his dear cause may sometimes hold. But that vice, if it were such, was the excess of a rare and splendid virtue, the use of the mind's eye and the mind's ear, eye of artist, ear of poet, where others had used only the dry comment and the compiling mind of the learned scholiast. Murray did not merely give his professional lectures: he took home to domestic sessions those with the sense to snatch at opportunity. A young scholar, who had perhaps been harassed and over-driven by the examination routine, after visiting Murray in the Woodstock Road (before the Boar's Hill days) would bicycle back to college in the rain through the sham Gothic of North Oxford feeling as though he had made a date with Aphrodite on the Parthenon. He had received new ears and eyes. Such is education. Murray's pupils were admitted to share his vision and to watch the primal, sudden, and superb thrust at civilisation which sprang from the waters of the Ionian Sea with the flash of the sword and the beauty of a flower. No less were they made to feel the pathos of that culture's withering and the desolation of its fall.

The career of George Gilbert Aimé Murray had been triumphs all the way. He was the third son of the late Sir Terence Aubrey Murray, President of the Legislative Council of New South Wales. At the age of eleven he left Australia to come to London, where he was educated at Merchant Taylors' School. Later he went to St John's College, Oxford—the University to which he was to return in later life laurelled with so many academic honours. His career can be summarised briefly: Fellow of New College, 1888; Professor of Greek at Glasgow University, 1889–99 (he was only twenty-three when Glasgow made the daring and brilliant choice); Professor of Greek at Oxford, 1908–36. In 1926 he was Charles Eliot Norton Professor of Poetry at Harvard. He was President of the International Committee of Intellectual Co-operation. His last and crowning honour came in 1941, when he received the Order of Merit.

Murray has been the scholar in action. The humanities of the study impelled him to be the humanist and humanitarian of liberal politics. He was associated especially with the League of Nations Union, of which he was Chairman for many years. Presiding over a committee this gentle scholar was less effective than on the lecturer's dais: chairmen need less reluctance to be summary and even wounding when bores are about. His zeal for the cause made him and many others of the faith somewhat blind to the weakness of the League as an instrument. But his energy and generosity were beyond praise, and none has given more personal devotion to the succouring of refugees and all distressed persons than the Murrays. At the age of twenty-three, when he went to Glasgow, he married Lady Mary Howard, daughter of the Earl of Carlisle, and it was a marriage of true minds and creeds, a long and noble partnership in the good works of civilisation and compassion.

In the theatre, too, he is not the scholar only. He wrote plays of his own and joined the brilliant group under Granville Barker which created the famous Court Theatre repertory. His translations of Euripides were staged by Barker with Lillah McCarthy and later by Lewis Casson and Sybil Thorndike: both in performance and in published form they reached a huge public. Over 50,000 copies of *Electra* were sold.

Not much given to pleasures of the table—Gilbert Murray is vegetarian and teetotaller—he has linked the feast of reason with the flow of soul. His studies in Greek Religion have been full of sympathy for the worshipper, fighting his way out of old savage terrors and taboos to some clear and gleaming vision of reason enthroned in law. Reading his translation of *The Bacchae* one decides that no confirmed water-drinker ever had more of the true spirit of Dionysos. His Hellenism unites the song of Pan with the Socratic wisdom and the politics of Pericles; it interprets:

> the hills olive-laden,
> Enchanted where first from the earth
> The grey-gleaming fruit of the Maiden
> Athena had birth;
> A soft grey crown for a city
> Beloved, a City of Light. . . .

In Murray classic and romantic become one: and rationalism becomes, beneath his hand, a lyric.

ARNOLD TOYNBEE

ARNOLD TOYNBEE is a name better known in America than in England. The Americans have built this professional historian into a prophet who may yet save Western civilisation. The abridged edition of his masterpiece, *A Study of History*, has lately become a best-seller in the United States, where a natural intellectual voracity is being sharpened by the anxieties of world-leadership.

In England his name often still evokes the question: 'Is he something to do with Toynbee Hall?'—except among the sophisticated, who will tell you that he is the moving influence behind the Foreign Office, a Roman Catholic or at least a Vatican fellow-traveller, and a reactionary in politics. All these are errors. It was his uncle who founded Toynbee Hall; he is a Protestant; at the last election he voted Common Wealth, which was as far Left as his constituency could offer; he has been one of the most prominent critics of British foreign policy, and in his relations with the Foreign Office he is much less like Keynes with the Treasury than Captain Shotover with the inhabitants of Heartbreak House.

He was born in 1889 (a week before Hitler) into one of the English intellectual dynasties. One uncle, Arnold, was the economist and historian; another, Paget, was the great Dante scholar; his grandfather was a distinguished surgeon; his mother herself wrote histories. Winchester, a Balliol scholarship, Classical Greats, an erudition even as an undergraduate that amazed and humbled such teachers as Sir Ernest Barker, a Balliol Fellowship in Ancient History, and marriage with Gilbert Murray's daughter completed the scholar's equipment in the liberal civilisation of Europe before the crash.

His three years as a don taught Toynbee that for him teaching and scholarship did not go together. It also taught his pupils that he knew far too much to be a good teacher. He could not begin to imagine the ignorance of others. In a sense this determined his life, because it led him to Chatham House. After a short spell as Professor of Byzantine and Modern Greek at London University, he became in 1925 Director of Studies at the newly-founded Institute of International Affairs.

Since then, Chatham House has been largely identified with Toynbee. There, unencumbered with undergraduates, he has written contemporary history in the annual *Survey of International Affairs*, and universal history in *A Study of History*. Either of these would have made his place among living historians secure; together they make it unique.

No great scholar ever had less intellectual arrogance. You are struck by the stooping figure, the white hair, the fine Grecian line from forehead to nose, but still more by the deference and charm with which he makes the conversation appear a privilege for himself instead of for you. Nor is this humility and sweetness the mask of a diplomatic intriguer. Toynbee's political characteristic is inaptitude, not ambition.

In 1914 he was swept like most intellectuals into Government service, which led to membership of the British delegation at the Peace Conference. In the second World War he again went into the Foreign Office, as Director of that group of Chatham House and other scholars which developed into the Foreign Office Research Department; and in 1946 he was once more on a British delegation to a Paris Peace Conference. Toynbee has valued the experience of public service as Gibbon valued the experience of a captain in the Hampshire Grenadiers.

But Toynbee was neither happy nor successful as a departmental head. His subordinates found that the intellectual virtue of being able to see every side of a question became the practical vice of irresolution. His place is not at the administrator's desk, still less behind the throne, but in the ivory tower. The war over, he gladly returned to Chatham House to edit the *Survey of International Affairs* for the war years, and to write the remaining three volumes of *A Study of History*, the *magnum opus*.

He began by thinking that religion existed for the sake of civilisation, but has become convinced that civilisation exists for the sake of religion. This view has made him the butt of both Marxists and 'realists', the two most popular schools of academic historians. A famous professor privately described *A Study of History* as 'unreadable fantasy'. 'A *de luxe* edition of *The Tablet*', said another. 'The only desert I have ever crossed for the sake of the oases', said a third. But Toynbee has the imperviousness to hostility of a gentle pachyderm. If his critics have anything constructive to say (it is surprising how seldom they do), their likeliest fate is to be embalmed verbatim, with courteous noises, in a prodigious footnote.

The motive of all Toynbee's writings has been interpreting the general breakdown through which his generation has lived. In his prophetic insight and objectivity he stands with the supreme historians of the nineteenth century—Acton, Burckhardt, and Tocqueville. As early as 1915, in his first book, he predicted that if Germany were deprived of the Polish Corridor it would occasion another war. In the same book he proposed that America should take over the administration of the Black Sea Straits. This famous suggestion came to nothing in 1919, but its ghost is the Truman Doctrine. In 1934 he foresaw America bestriding a prostrate Japan.

Some will take this as evidence that Toynbee lurks under Mr Marshall's bed as well as Mr Bevin's. It is the vulgar delusion of those who do not understand how intellectual activity can be disinterested. Toynbee's peculiarity as a historian is not in his influence on events; the only notice of him that the events have ever taken is to follow the least desirable of the alternative courses he has predicted.

BENEDETTO CROCE

THE first open Congress held during the war on the European Continent by political parties born underground in the fight against Nazi-Fascism was dominated by a Conservative. This may seem a paradox, but it has an easy political explanation.

Benedetto Croce, the philosopher who was the first speaker at the Congress of Bari in January, 1944, and gave the lead, had been, during the last forty years, one of the world's loftiest exponents of traditional thought. It was mainly as a conserver of tradition that he warned both the Allies and the Italians of the dangers arising from 'their negations and their delay in keeping the promise to extirpate Fascism in Italy'. He said:

> The people of other European countries are looking to Italy as the first land freed from Fascism and Nazism and a first example of the new life. Any lasting or temporary compromise with dictatorship, either open or hidden, is dangerous and must be dismissed. Liberty, through tolerant discussion, must be our counsellor, and guarantee social stability as liberty and tolerance alone can do. Authoritarian régimes, whatever their name or disguise, are not conservative. They impoverish the social forces, rouse inefficiency and apathy, open the way to weariness and disorder, and provoke revolutions.

Benedetto Croce was born in 1866 at Pescasseroli, in the very core of the Abruzzi mountains, some ten miles north of the difficult central point of the present Italian front.

After having completed his secondary school education in a Catholic college at Naples, Croce found himself 'outside the faith'; at Rome University, where he studied for a few terms, he was a pupil of the Italian apostle of Marx, the sociologist Arturo Labriola, the only one of his teachers whom he really loved and admired; nevertheless Croce soon repudiated the foundations of Marxism and, instead of taking a degree, wrote a still widely studied critical essay on Marx.

BENEDETTO CROCE

A considerable family fortune allowed him financial independence from Universities and Academies. His family had been for a century prominent in the civic affairs of Naples, the capital of the Southern Kingdom before the *Risorgimento*. When Benedetto was seventeen, both his parents and his only sister were killed by an earthquake in Ischia. He himself remained buried under the débris for several hours, and received severe injuries. He was taken care of in the Roman household of his uncles, Silvio and Bertrando Spaventa, the first an able financier and administrator, the second a distinguished Hegelian philosopher. So young Benedetto had plenty of good tuition in the philosophy of the spirit and actualities of public life.

Today, many classify Croce as a Hegelian. Hegel impressed the young Croce first through his interpretation of art as an integral part of history, so much in contrast to the interpretation of the moralist Kant, in whose system art was left but as a hobby, and to that of the sociologist Marx, who regarded art as irrelevant.

It is not a mere chance that the first volume of Croce's *General Theory of the Spirit* is called *Aesthetics*. It puts forward a theory later condensed and slightly developed by himself under this title in the *Encyclopædia Britannica*. He argued that, amid the continuous change of history, there is something permanent in the human spirit which allows men to talk with each other and understand each other across the centuries. Disbelief in the purely 'economic man' made him a moralist. On moral grounds he rejected revolutions. But, unlike many other Conservatives, he regards revolutions as consequences of immoral situations. His condemnation of régimes which bring about revolutions or try to bridle and prevent them with illegal means, is not less violent than his condemnation of revolution itself. Freedom, in fact, is to him a supreme guarantee and link of the inseparable ideas of tradition and evolution, thanks to which humanity can march to new goals while consistent with itself.

Croce was made a politician by his passion for goodness and

knowledge. In the early years after the last war the bulky, thoughtful, and vivacious Southern philosopher became Minister of Education in Giolitti's cabinet, and prepared a measure of reform designed to rid Italian education of the materialist mentality which had dominated it before the war, and which—according to Croce—has proved fallacious not only in Italy but also in other countries; the very fact that war broke in a world which believed in universal peace through material advancement was striking enough. When Mussolini came to power and declared that he agreed with Croce's thought, the philosopher did not oppose the régime at first. However, after the Matteotti crime and the ensuing rise against Fascism, the constitutional guarantees of liberty were withdrawn from the people, and Fascism showed its true face: disorder and lawlessness were supreme.

Even when the dictatorship triumphed and he could no longer openly condemn the régime, he expounded his union of liberty and of tradition, not so much a political programme but an ethical way of thinking and living.

Small wonder that, in the general Fascist darkness, hundreds of intelligent young men from all over the country came to see the Neapolitan philosopher; even smaller wonder that now, towards the end of his scholarly and upright career, Croce is the dominating figure among the various democratic parties. The old anti-Marxian has paid homage to the Soviets who built a new stability in place of the self-destroying tyranny of the Tsars. The old agnostic wrote a recent article entitled, *Why We call Ourselves Christians*. To mingle innovation and tradition and both with tolerance and justice is the aesthetic as well as the practice of this great man. He has long been revered in the universities of the world and now he stands before the larger public as the first citizen of his country who, like Signor Benedick, 'goes foremost in report through Italy'.

C. G. JUNG

TIME was when modern psychology had to endure abuse; today it has 'arrived', and much of its terminology has seeped through into common usage.

Professor C. G. Jung was, and still is, in the vanguard of this development, so that one cannot consider him apart from his work. At the age of seventy-four he is the last of the trio, Freud, Jung, and Adler, to remain alive—alive and still producing original work in considerable volume.

The son of a Swiss pastor and philologist, Jung started his career as a psychiatrist at the Burghölzli Asylum, in Zurich; Bleuler was his teacher. There he became one of that small group of men who were transforming psychiatry from an exercise in classification to a dynamic, interpretative science. Their aim was to see how far mental illness could be not merely treated empirically but understood, and their efforts have resounded throughout the world.

It was during this period at the Burghölzli that Jung succeeded in peering behind the façade of everyday life to unveil the hidden forces of the unconscious. He and not Freud, as is usually thought, first used the term 'complex' to indicate those knots of emotionally toned ideas or feelings which he found disturbing the surface of consciousness. It was this discovery which led him first to champion Freud, at the risk of his professional career, then to meet him and later to collaborate with him.

Jung and Freud will always be coupled together, and probably with justice, even though their work is in many respects so different. For about six years they worked together closely, even analysing each other's dreams. But Jung could never have continued simply as a psychoanalyst, if only because the lines of his own development were laid down in his earliest work. Freud and he parted company. Freud had hoped Jung would follow him as the leader of psychoanalysis and was disappointed. Jung certainly regarded his work as a legitimate contribution to the new young science which Freud had founded, but his work was not accepted, and so he was to continue his own way alone.

At this time Jung was greatly impressed by the inability of psychotherapists to agree amongst themselves; not only he, but also Alfred Adler, had been unable to collaborate with Freud. He saw the difficulty in terms of differences of temperament, and this idea was a potent factor in—though not the only source of origin for—the development of his theory of types. The extravert and the introvert have conflicted throughout history—they still do so today. Jung saw Freud as the extravert and Adler as the introvert.

Though the 'complex' and the type problem are the best-known features of Jung's work, he will probably be longest remembered for his theory of the collective unconscious, that vast reservoir of life and wisdom which man has within his nature, but of which he is only too liable to become the instrument instead of the master, with disastrous consequences.

His theory of the collective unconscious gave him not only a particular interest in the psychology of the masses but also a strong reason for travelling. As a Swiss he would naturally know France, Germany, Austria and Italy; he has often been to Britain, and has paid several visits to the United States. India he found specially attractive, whilst his interest in primitive psychology took him to Africa, where he lived for some time among the coloured peoples. All these journeys would never have come about without his researches and discoveries in Zurich, for Jung is an introvert, and has discovered the world, as it were, from within himself. The primitive, the oriental, the European, and the American are, for him, all manifestations of the central unit, man.

Jung's enormous capacity for work (as a writer he is amazingly prolific) has made it possible for him to master a bewildering variety of subjects. He is a good classical scholar, has an almost unparalleled knowledge of mythology, knows and speaks four languages idiomatically, and at least two others fairly well. He has indeed been accused of putting his name to the work of others, since he could not possibly know so much himself!

With all his abilities and knowledge, however, he is human in the best sense. He is a married man (his wife is also an analyst) and has five healthy normal children, a fact of particular significance, since Jung has always laid the abnormalities of children at the parents' door. Today his five children have produced nineteen grandchildren; they all live in Zurich and infest Jung's house and garden. He can be excellent company by ordinary standards, is fond of good food and wine, and has a great capacity for enjoying himself. He has a broad sense of humour, and those who go to see the 'great psychologist' may find themselves, as one visitor said, confronted by 'a rough peasant'. But he has the failings of the introvert, especially in relation to the world, where he is apt to get into hot water through being too outspoken. He is not good at organising and has never attempted, like Freud, to build up an organisation to develop his theories.

To his house by the Lake of Zurich men and women have come from all over the world—psychologists, scholars, scientists, business men, artists, politicians—and because he is a brilliant linguist and a classical scholar, as well as a scientist, he is able to meet them and to understand the diversity of human nature perhaps better than any other man in the world. Because of his exceptional experience he is difficult to pigeonhole: he has been called mystic, philosopher, prophet. But in reality it is not so complicated; the facts of human psychology are always his primary concern.

These facts led Jung to conclude as early as 1918 that Western civilisation as a whole was passing through a radical and dangerous period of moral crisis, owing to disturbances in the activity of the collective unconscious, and he at that time named Germany as the most probable next centre of danger. His conclusions have received sufficient confirmation to make us realise there is a real basis for his picture of recent and contemporary events, and, though he does not give us much consolation, he at least has a diagnosis worthy of serious consideration.

Jung is almost the last remaining European scientist of his generation. But does he belong only to his generation? In a sense he is timeless, and to many he points the way to the future—to the future man who will grasp realities with super-human objectivity, while remaining conscious of ordinary human weakness.

THOMAS MANN

BUDDENBROOKS, the work that established Thomas Mann's fame, was perhaps the most extraordinary first novel ever written. It was a masterpiece; it was a prototype; it was of epic dimensions and yet free from *longueurs*; it was written in a detached, objective manner, and in a spirit of ironically resigned pessimism; all in all, it was a remarkably premature work.

The first of many family sagas, it appeared in 1900; it depicted, with rare invention and character-creation, the world and society of liberal bourgeois culture, then at the height of its splendour, prosperity, and confidence; and with quiet and sad prophetic insight, rang its knell.

Thomas Mann had started writing *Buddenbrooks* when he was hardly more than twenty—a youth from a good Hanseatic family, but now poor and turned loose on the world, living a Bohemian life in Munich and Rome. For more than three years he secretly and busily worked away, in cheap boarding-house rooms, at the richly growing, strange, secreted work; then he sent the only existing handwritten manuscript to a publisher. It narrowly missed a rejection, but was finally printed; immediately Mann found himself famous.

The success of *Buddenbrooks* had a certain power to stun. It cut short a literary career which had hardly begun, by overwhelming a young and unknown author at once with all the prizes that come, as a rule, in maturity. It brutally tore him from creative and protective obscurity into the fierce and sterilising light of publicity. It labelled him: even to the literary world, let alone the broad reading public, Thomas Mann was from now on the author of *Buddenbrooks*, the classical chronicler of bourgeoisie, from whom nothing else was to be expected, or even willingly accepted.

As for himself, he was for a while left astonished. One thing soon became clear: he was not going to turn out another *Buddenbrooks*. He never did the same thing twice. For more than ten years he wrote only slender works, and only few of them; highly polished and slightly artificial long short stories, usually treating—and bitterly questioning—the rôle of the artist in society. By 1914, when he was forty, many critics secretly considered him a spent force. His brother Heinrich, in a fierce literary quarrel, could aim this shaft at him: 'The mark of those who are to dry up early is to appear objective and worldly wise in their youth.'

At that time Thomas Mann had before him both his real literary achievement and the political drama of his personal life.

He was still to write those two great epics which outrange and dwarf even *Buddenbrooks*—*The Magic Mountain*, that profound criticism of twentieth-century Europe and its ideologies, and the high, metaphysical comedy of *Joseph and his Brethren*. With their retinue of attendant shorter novels, short stories and essays, these two enormous works are sometimes held to be the greatest individual literary achievement of our time; for comparison, one has to go outside our century, to such bodies of work as those of Milton, or Goethe, or Tolstoi.

Their adventurous sweep and perspective, their exciting combination of boldness in conception and neatness in execution, are there for all to see and enjoy. What is hidden from the reader of the English translations is the miracle that in these works was wrought on the German language. As a literary medium, the German language has been in a steady decline since about 1890. In these works of the mature Thomas Mann, however, it not only regains the baroque richness and mysterious warmth of Goethe's and Stifter's prose, but acquires in addition a supple plasticity and precision which it hardly ever had before. The wonder is that many pages of such fine German prose were written in the U.S.A., by a man who had become an American citizen, lived in English-speaking surroundings, and had himself, in his advanced years, taken to English for daily use, reserving German only as his 'ritual language'.

This leads to the personal story of Thomas Mann's later life—that highly controversial story which has done as much as his early, blinding success to impede a just appreciation of his work.

OBSERVER PROFILES

For the broad international newspaper-reading public, the name of Thomas Mann today stands not for the profound and distinctive literary workmanship which it will probably signify to posterity. It is merely the name of a famous German who broke with Germany in the days of Hitler. Thomas Mann was not alone in that. The strange thing about him is that in the first World War he was perhaps the most eloquent literary apologist of the German cause—and yet in the end, when he at last reluctantly broke with his native country, the break was final.

Thomas Mann is not a Toscanini who enthusiastically returned to his Italy once it was freed from Mussolini. Thomas Mann has become an American citizen. More: he has become an American patriot, an ardent believer in, and propagator of, America's pacifying and civilising world mission. A man born with a peculiar talent for patriotism and a bent for zealous and militant love of country, he has succeeded, late in his life, in transferring that love whole from one country to another—a curious, moving, and slightly bewildering thing to do, and a worthy subject of a novel by Thomas Mann himself. Indeed, if one comes to think of it, some of the process has been described in the closing volumes of his novel, *Joseph and his Brethren*, when he tells how Joseph became an Egyptian.

Apart from this, the long, painful journey round the political horizon, which Thomas Mann performed between 1914 and 1945, has left as its residue something like a second body of work—five or six strong volumes of political essays, articles, and speeches, accompanying world history since 1914 like a highly subjective running commentary, given from an ever-moving platform. They start with those long, ponderous, but still in part startlingly persuasive *Meditations of a Nonpolitical Man*, in which Thomas Mann, during the 1914-18 war, so fervently polemicised against democracy, and praised that freedom from politics which is vouchsafed by authoritarian government. They end—for the time being—with the wartime talks over the German Service of the B.B.C., propagating the cause of democracy to a hostile Germany.

THOMAS MANN

How many stations are there in between! The hesitant peace of a loyal Monarchist with the Weimar Republic; the decorous wooing of France, in the name of official Germany; the magisterial and patriotic warnings against rising National Socialism; the final break with Germany in the scathing letter to the Dean of Bonn University; the discovery of America; the discovery of democracy; the mounting horror and wrath at the outrages committed by Germany and Germans during the war; the refusal to relent; the slow relenting. . . .

This strange secondary work of Thomas Mann will probably prove more perishable than his epic novels. Thomas Mann is not a creative political thinker; through all his political writings he really remains the 'non-political man', emotional, brilliant in his literary advocacy, somewhat too easily carried away, touching in a sincerity which sometimes leads him to indiscretion. The political student will find little to learn in Thomas Mann's political writings. The literary connoisseur will find something to enjoy in them, though less than in the novels and stories. The real gainer will be the biographer, to whom they present the living record of the moving personal drama of a great man.

T. S. ELIOT

ANDREW ELIOT, a cordwainer, born in 1627, left the Somerset village of East Coker in middle age to go to America. Thomas Stearns Eliot returned to that spot (via Messrs Faber and Faber) in 1940.

The poem *East Coker* begins with the words 'in my beginning is my end': it ends with the words 'in my end is my beginning'. But in between? In between were generations in Boston and an unbroken communication with learning and with heaven which may have infringed even the supposed celestial monopoly of the Lowells or the Cabots.

The Eliot family had a dignified and austere ecclesiastical and academic tradition. (The grandfather of 'T. S.' established Washington University.) His mother, descendant of Isaac Stearns, an original settler of 1630, composed a dramatic poem, *Savonarola*, to which Thomas, her seventh and youngest, has written a pious filial preface. He has regained for the family, if they had ever lost it, an impeccable English—a new English—accent. The official assumption of English nationality in 1927 was redundant by exactly 300 years—the precise date is, surely, not by chance: and exactly twenty-one years later, he has the O.M.

Whether the honour is exclusively literary—as fellow poets would prefer—is problematical: it might also be political, a gesture to America, since this heir of a Bostonian tradition was born at St Louis and had part of his peripatetic education at Harvard, as well as in Oxford and Paris. It might also be ecclesiastical—as fellow Bishops should not deny. For Eliot, who, unlike most natives of St Louis, proclaims himself Royalist and High Church, is naturally an Arch-poet and temperamentally a major Bishop. The extent to which his style is founded upon the Authorised Version has been overlooked by his critics.

No poet and critic of his standing before him has been more rigidly careful to let out nothing unauthorised. There has been no hint of rashness or scandal in his judgment of contemporaries. This gives weight to his critical authority. At the same time he has been radical in his assessment of classics. He has

T. S. ELIOT

impugned Milton, which made him liable to some stinging rebukes, and he has said of *Hamlet*: 'So far from being Shakespeare's masterpiece the play is an artistic failure.' At the same time Eliot has founded a new poetic tradition in the theatre, a feat of genius, and his two plays, *Murder in the Cathedral* and *The Family Reunion*, have raised the temperature of more theatres than the Mercury almost to fever point. (Incidentally, the title *Murder in the Cathedral*, obviously good box-office, was not his own invention.) It is interesting to notice that his first book of poems, *Prufrock and Other Observations*, was published in 1917 in the same year as *Tradition and the Individual Talent*, perhaps his most important critical statement, was delivered. Both came early: both are middle-aged, finished, original work. Mr Eliot has indeed relied upon being upper-middle-aged, and upper-middle-class, all his life.

Having, as a travelling scholar, known pre-1914 Europe and having consumed its tradition with exquisite greed, he returned briefly to America—and then returned to a Europe in apocalyptic ruin. Wavering between the profit of America and the loss of Europe, he chose Europe, if positive choice it were: Europe already had chosen him. He saw this European world from abundant angles, as bank official, schoolmaster, and editor. His command of the literary review, *The Criterion*, never failed the proud claim of its title.

He had arrived back with the seventeenth-century style which Andrew Eliot had taken with him. But it was a style revealing a profound sea-change. Here was something as new to language as the application of electricity; and this impact upon the vocabulary of poetry was immense, and increases. Eliot created the poetic style of the twentieth century; again, a feat of genius. And it is, one might say, personal and ancestral. This he did here, in England, almost by instinct. For his means of expression, poetry is wholly natural to him; his rhythms are original and innate, as the rhythms of all true poets are. He is often so allusive as to be elusive, but the essential quality of the poetry transcends the intellectual snobbishness of his method and the elephantine tip-toeing of his expositors.

OBSERVER PROFILES

There is no monotony about him. In the same year he produced books on *The Idea of a Christian Society* and *Practical Cats*. In a comic poem he describes himself with his:

> . . . brow so grim
> And his mouth so prim
> And his conversation so nicely
> Restricted to What Precisely
> And If and Perhaps and But—

How unpleasant, he says, *to meet Mr Eliot.* But the opposite is the case. For it is enchanting to meet this self-doubtful, modest person, so gloriously ready to laugh with a most unexpected kind of yaffling sound. He is not so much a don as a college—where on any staircase Professor Channing-Cheetah may have the room below Sweeney, and where a bell called Medium Tom tolls precisely and with a dead stroke on the sound of forty-nine. But he has created a new respect for the mystery of poetry; he has done for words what he would do for The Word—and in *The Four Quartets* these two aims are triumphantly brought together.

It is possible to divide his work into two. The unfinished *Sweeney Agonistes*—perhaps his masterpiece had he finished it —is the turning point in his development as a poet: it is his last look back at the Waste Land of the world he was leaving; yet it is as near as he has ever got to humanity. For an instant the Edgware Road in which he lived escapes, becomes unauthorised, impolitic, at first-hand.

Mr Eliot is eminently—one can use the word without a hint of cliché—eminently respectable. He has made no literary enemies but many unseen opponents; a few unseen friends but many public worshippers. Through his influence he has been the occasion of a mass of appalling verse and the cause of a portion of true poetry. In his capacity as publisher he has been able to exclude and to accept; there may be a hint of bias for his fellow churchmen, but that is a welcome sign of human frailty. Father Eliot has indeed heard confession of contemporary poetry more often than any other, and must have discovered some pretty odd things in the process. Whether his influence as a poet will be as lasting as the present imitation of him tends to suggest, none of us can live to see. Lacking the self-confidence of Enoch Soames or the professional skill of Madame Sosostris one cannot attempt to 'haruspicate or scry'. Everyone has his own idea of the greatest living poet, but that Eliot is the most famous living poet perhaps only he himself would be found to doubt.

TRANSATLANTIC

HENRY WALLACE

IN leaving the Democratic Party to found a new Third Party, Henry Wallace is following a pattern of non-conformity which is almost stereotyped in his family. A distant ancestor in Ireland left the respectable Episcopal Church to become a Presbyterian solely because the State was persecuting Presbyterians; Henry himself has abandoned the Presbyterian Church, in which so many of his forebears preached hellfire, to rejoin the Episcopal Church, which in his native Iowa is amongst the poorest and least 'respectable' of congregations.

Similarly in politics Wallace came to manhood as a staunch Republican during the eight years of Wilson's Democratic administration, but, when the Republicans triumphed at last and his father became President Harding's Secretary of Agriculture, young Henry was afflicted with doubts which resulted in his becoming a Democrat. As it turned out this was to his advantage for when the Democrats were swept to power under Roosevelt, he became Secretary of Agriculture, and introduced that intricate system of price supports under which the American farmer still operates. His success won him the cupboard love of the farmers, the devotion of his department, and the abiding admiration of the President.

In 1940 Mr Roosevelt, much against the party's will, chose Wallace as his Vice-President, so that he came to preside over the most select club in the world—the American Senate. The visionary qualities which appealed to the President, aroused distrust amongst Senators. A friendly member once thought to impress some sceptics by asking Wallace how he had managed to make himself a fortune out of breeding hybrid corn; 'Because I have a deep sympathy for plants', was the studied reply.

Wallace finds people harder to get on with than plants, and his shyness has always been a handicap to him as a public speaker. A few years ago he became interested in mass hypnotism as an aid to dealing with crowds, but somewhere the careful plan went awry for it now appears that Wallace becomes hypnotised by the crowds. It has always been true that he could not deal with hostile audiences, but more recently he has come to sense with exquisite feeling the sentiment of his audience and then say exactly what they want to hear. The family capacity for preaching hellfire has not been lost, but now the congregation is always saved, the hellfire is reserved for those outside. Thus in 1946, in an address to an extreme Left Wing group in New York, the passages critical of Russia and Communism, which appeared in the text, unaccountably disappeared from the spoken word, while the denunciation of Britain was given to the cheering echo. Yet, a few weeks later, speaking in London, his praise of Britain was only matched by his denunciation of America, and, though a stranger in Britain, his *rapport* with the audience was so perfect that many of his hearers felt that his speech might almost have been written in the office of his host—*The New Statesman*.

Apart from the Bible the book Henry Wallace is most fond of quoting is Sir Charles Petrie's *Revolutions of Civilisation*, which he read when he was a youth. It has taught him the impermanence of great cultures; the necessity of their decline and fall, the inevitability of their replacement by new, more vigorous ways of life. Enthralled by these philosophic reflections on the millennia, Wallace has for so long scanned the horizon to glimpse the dawn of a new era, that he finds it hard to focus on the light and shade of more immediate happenings. The crash of 1929 sounded to his ready ear like the last trump of the American way of life, and he looked—in the words of his favourite text—for 'a new heaven and new earth'. For a time it really seemed as if the New Deal was indeed what Wallace termed it, 'a New Testament of Democracy', and its messiah was Roosevelt.

Even the fervour of this new faith could not prevent Wallace's receptive mind from seeking other new and unknown gods. Exponents of Yogi, Buddhism, Zoroastoranism and less ordinary cults were frequent visitors at his office. As Secretary of Agriculture he tried to get recognition for a Red Indian medicine man who had a new method of rainmaking, but as Vice-President it was Wallace who asked Roosevelt to listen to Einstein's plea that the United States Government should finance an even wilder project, which produced the atom bomb. New projects of every sort—new diets, such as a remarkably anti-social one based on garlic; new sports, such as the lone game of throwing boomerangs—made Wallace the White Knight of the New Deal. But as the war clouds deepened his conviction that a great new age was at hand, and his fear that New Deal Americanism was not enough grew upon him, Wallace became more and more misanthropic. With the fall of France in June 1940, the fortunes of civilised mankind seemed at their nadir—the following night Wallace talked by radio to the nation on 'the strength and quietness of grass'.

After a year of travail in which the world seemed to be giving birth to nothing new, Wallace's gloom began to be lifted by hearing about the new civilisation of America's recent ally Russia. The Vice-President avidly devoured the report of radical friends who were returning to favour after a long exile, and in 1942 he made a famous speech on Russia in which he coined a phrase 'The New Democracy'. His enthusiasm for this fresh faith in which 'Russia, perceiving some of the abuses of excessive political democracy, has placed strong emphasis on economic democracy' knew no bounds. The New Democracy replaced the New Deal as the hope of the world; but who was to be its messiah?

At this moment, by a strange coincidence, the clearest stigmata of messiahdom—persecution—began to afflict Henry Wallace. He quarrelled over economic warfare with the most conservative member of the Cabinet—Jesse Jones—and was publicly humiliated by the President who replaced him as chairman of the Board of Economic Warfare by James F. Byrnes. Shortly after this Byrnes and Jones conspired to oust Wallace from the Vice-Presidency at the 1944 convention, and he was replaced by Harry Truman.

Wallace did not have to wait long for his revenge. In January 1945, in return for his continued loyalty to Roosevelt, he demanded and received Jesse Jones' post as Secretary of Commerce. In March Mr Byrnes suddenly retired into private life. In April . . . Harry Truman, who had supplanted him as heir to the Presidency, succeeded to the White House; four months later Byrnes returned as Secretary of State. Such buffets at the hands of man and fate only strengthened Wallace's belief in his own rightness, and the futility of his opponents. In September 1946, by attacking his cabinet colleague Byrnes in a public speech, Wallace forced Mr Truman to choose between his Secretary of State and his Secretary of Commerce. As a result, after fourteen years, Henry Wallace went back into opposition.

This bed of affliction has proved surprisingly soft. Wallace has found numerous and extremely helpful disciples, only too anxious to bear him up lest he dash his mind against a fact. The old difficulty with speeches has quite disappeared; friends are more than kind in aiding their composition, halls are never empty, audiences are never apathetic, always enthusiastic. Wherever he goes the leader of the new party is always surrounded by friends, eager to tell him what is happening in the world, how greatly he is now respected, how darkly envied by his enemies, late colleagues. For instance, in his European tour Wallace was surprised to find nothing but strong support for his views 'except from the reactionaries around Winston Churchill'; true, the newspapers suggested a different picture, but who believes the capitalist press if he has friends to tell him the truth? In this new bright light all is clear, all is simple, conflicts disappear and friendship reigns. 'I want Russia to make a tremendous success of Communism', says Henry Wallace. 'I wish I could see the *Politburo* face to face to show them that it is to the welfare of Russia that the United States should make a success of capitalism.' So the Gideon's army, the column of the New Democracy, marches on and at its head its leader, the new messiah, is carried forward on a wave of friendship, his feet never touching the ground.

SENATOR VANDENBERG

THE pilot of the Marshall Plan through the tempestuous seas of congressional politics was 'the Man from Michigan', Senator Arthur Hendrik Vandenberg.

To have full charge of the most ambitious and enlightened programme of internationalism in modern times is a strange reversal of fortune for someone who was counted a leading isolationist at the time of Pearl Harbour. His conversion was first made evident only a few years ago, on 10 January 1945, when he startled the American Senate by proposing that America should offer a guarantee in Europe and Asia against any renewal of Axis aggression.

Because of his isolationist Republican record this speech created far more turmoil than similar speeches by established interventionists. 'There's been nothing like it in modern times', is the Senator's own characteristic comment on the public reaction. The importance of Vandenberg's present position as President *pro tem.* of the Senate and chairman of the Foreign Affairs Committee is difficult to exaggerate, though the Senator sometimes succeeds in doing so.

But if his pleasure at the status he has obtained is sometimes less than modest, Vandenberg has the excuse that he has achieved his special ambition in attaining the position held by two men he hero-worshipped—Senator Lodge, who, as chairman of the Foreign Relations Committee, defeated the Versailles Treaty, and Senator Borah, who, from the same post in the 'thirties, led the fight for isolation.

The outbreak of war in 1939 came two months after Borah had denied its possibility, but though the war was an undeniable fact, at least he could firmly assert it was not America's war. But the strongest emotion Vandenberg knows is patriotism; not the flag-wagging patriotism endemic amongst politicians, but a deep and abiding, almost mystical, affection for the United States. The threat to his country's safety in 1940–42 made the Senator seriously question the validity of the thesis of 'insulation' in which he had been brought up, to defend which he had written a book, and on which issue he had recently been re-elected.

Somewhat of a stranger in the field of internationalism, he looked outside the Senate for advice. Perhaps he got some from his personal friend and next door neighbour, Henry Wallace; certainly he got much from the *New York Times* diplomatic expert, 'Scotty' Reston. The result was that in his sixtieth year, and his sixteenth in the Senate, this respectable unimaginative politician broke with the isolationist beliefs of his whole career, of his mentors and friends, and of his party. It was an act to compare with Gladstone's conversion to Home Rule at the age of seventy-six.

President Roosevelt at once recognised an ally in his struggle to make America aware of her world responsibilities, and appointed Vandenberg an American delegate to the San Francisco conference which drew up the Charter of the United Nations.

At San Francisco Vandenberg grew from being an unimportant mid-Western Senator into a world figure. With only the faint regrets of an actor who hears the insistent cry for yet another curtain call, he says: 'I can't say a word now that does not bring out microscopes all over the world'.

The laurels of an elder statesman fit Vandenberg as well as his Senatorial toga. He is the sort of man a Hollywood producer would choose to play the part of an American Senator: he struts rather than walks; he orates rather than talks; and when he gets home he laughs at himself for doing both, or, if he forgets to laugh at himself, his amiable self-effacing wife laughs at him. In his suite at the Wardman Park Hotel Vandenberg is allowed to feel as important as he likes—but not divine. When he relaxes he relaxes thoroughly; the rather owlish dignity of his face becomes amiably paternal, he chats about trivia with his children, or sinks into the sofa and re-reads his favourite mysteries by Sax Rohmer.

The outward Senatorial pomposity has its origins in the time when, as a stripling of twenty-two, young Vandenberg was asked to become editor and publisher of his home town newspaper—the *Grand Rapids Herald*. At the time he was only a reporter, but in his endeavour to support his parents he had held many jobs before, including running a stamp exchange and trying to patent 'Titan Tabules for Seasickness'.

OBSERVER PROFILES

The owner of the paper, Senator Smith, gave Arthur Vandenberg complete control of the paper, and for twenty-three years he daily wrote its editorials and directed a staff composed at first largely of his elders. He gave himself the slightly ridiculous airs of middle age to avoid appearing ridiculously young; but when he went to the Senate for Michigan at the age of forty-five the airs had become habitual and were regarded as something of a joke by his colleagues.

The task of creating a bipartisan foreign policy has not been easy. After the San Francisco conference the Senator travelled constantly with the Secretary of State—his old Senatorial colleague Jimmy Byrnes. Then when intimacy was established, so that even the victory of the Republicans in the 1946 elections could not shake it, Byrnes made way for Marshall. The easygoing Byrnes' days of glasses of whisky in hotel room conferences were replaced by formal lunches in the cold atmosphere of the official Blair House. But good will and some involuntary match-making by Molotov rewove the pattern, and Vandenberg is as close to Marshall today as he was to Byrnes before.

As close—but not too close; for the strength of the bipartisan foreign policy is that Republicans do not feel that their representative is the rubber stamp of a Democratic State Department. They know that Vandenberg has pressed on a reluctant Secretary of State the necessity of closer relations with Perón's Argentina and with Chiang Kai-shek's China. It is history that he wrote vital amendments into the United Nations Charter and into the 'Truman Doctrine' on Greece and Turkey. It is generally accepted that from the end of 1945 it was Vandenberg who stiffened the State Department against Russia and it was his statement that 'I can co-operate with only one Secretary of State at a time' that forced Truman to drop Henry Wallace from his Cabinet for criticising this firm policy.

Vandenberg's place in history is secure. For, overshadowed though he has been by Roosevelt and Marshall, it is the patriotic, vain, shrewd, oratorical 'Man from Michigan' who has enabled the United States at last to play its proper rôle as a great Power, by ensuring bipartisan support for its Foreign Policy.

JOHN L. LEWIS

WHATEVER one may think of Mr Lewis's ideas and actions, there has been no sort of doubt that, since the death of Samuel Gompers, the founder and first president of the American Federation of Labour, he has been the outstanding figure in the American trade union movement.

There are not, indeed, half a dozen figures in American public life who are better known to the man-in-the-street. Right or wrong, he is a dominating and masterful person. He has all the natural gifts of a leader, the instinct to dominate, the will to the initiative, and interest in the dynamics of organisation, a love of the limelight. Restless, daring, resourceful, nothing but his fantastic vanity could prevent him from being a very great man. But he cannot brook opposition, and he always assumes that an intellectual difference is a personal injury. So that though he has a remarkable power of evoking loyalty it is rare for the loyalty to be continuous in any man with a will of his own.

Mr Lewis always wants subordinates; he has never wanted colleagues. The result is that, though he has probably greater gifts than any leader so far thrown up by the American Labour Movement, he is unlikely to leave the decisive mark that he ought, granted their level, to have made.

Mr Lewis's career divides itself, rather naturally, into three periods. Up to the New Deal he was a typical miners' leader, an orthodox Republican in outlook, notable for his power as an organiser, aggressive, even brutal, to his enemies, showing no sign of difference from a score of other trade union leaders.

Then came what seemed almost like a religious conversion. The Great Depression seemed to change the essentials of his character. He made claims for the American working man which outstripped the archaic principles of the Federation of Labour. When the latter refused to find a place for those claims, he broke with it and founded, with a group of faithful lieutenants, the Committee of Industrial Organisations.

That breach marked an epoch in American economic history. For, in its remarkable progress, he proved not only that the C.I.O. could organise those unskilled workers to whom the A.F. of L. had paid scant attention in the past; he proved, also, that the 'white collar' worker was capable of organisation.

And from 1933 until the famous 'sit-down' strikes of 1937 he was more influential than any American Labour leader has been, both in securing recognition from employers in industries previously adamant against collective bargaining, and in securing from the Roosevelt Administration legislation more favourable to the claims of Labour than any other figure had obtained.

In these years he seemed almost as much a prophet as an organiser. No influence counted more than his in swinging the Labour vote overwhelmingly to Mr Roosevelt in 1936.

But, about mid-way in the President's second term, a change became evident once more in his temper. It was clear that he expected more concessions than he received. A critical note began to emerge in his utterances. By 1939 it was obvious that he was in opposition; and in 1940 there was no more zealous opponent of the third term. When the C.I.O. refused to follow him in his support of Mr Wilkie, he not only resigned from its leadership but took with him the United Mine Workers, whose strength had been the foundation of the C.I.O.

When Mr Roosevelt was re-elected, he had worked himself into a fury with the President and all his policies. He luxuriated in fury against the President, against England, even against those who had served him as devoted colleagues in the C.I.O.; it was typical of that fury that he should persuade, or compel, the United Mine Workers to expel Mr Philip Murray, his successor as leader of the C.I.O., from membership of the union to which Mr Murray had given the devotion of half a lifetime.

His action in bringing out the miners on strike in the middle of war for an extra two dollars a day, though very largely justified by the conditions of the mining industry in the United States, was probably not less a deliberate affirmation of his importance in the economic life of America than it was an effort to improve the conditions of his men. That effort was rather an effect than a cause of his inexhaustible will to power.

JOHN L. LEWIS

It is impossible not to be impressed by Mr Lewis. The great head, with its fierce eyes and heavy brows, is the index to a man of massive personality. He has big ideas and he has inexhaustible courage. He has done a remarkable job for millions of American workers whom traditional trade unionism had failed to reach. They have rewarded him with a salary of 25,000 dollars a year as well as their loyalty. But his vanity traps him. It has transformed a man who once looked as though he might be among the most creative Americans of his time into a man to whom hardly any political cause is wrong if its service enables him to hit back at those who have wounded his vanity.

After almost a decade, in which it seemed possible that he would build an American trade union movement of incomparable strength, he has become again the John L. Lewis he was before the Great Depression. He retains his daring and his relentless will to power. But he has lost his sense of perspective, his creative imagination, and the chance he seemed to have of an achievement unrivalled in the history of trade unionism.

He is bound, by the power he commands, to exercise a great influence; but he has sacrificed his chance of shaping the American future to the passion for blowing his own trumpet.

WALT DISNEY

IT is the fashion among elders these days to find Disney a 'disappointment', as no doubt the elders of James the First's days found the established, carelessly munificent Shakespeare a disappointment. But the young still love him. With the instinctive wisdom of childhood, they feel he is of their own kind.

No tribute could please Walt Disney more. An intensely shy, worrying, and rather inarticulate man, he is never quite at his ease with grown-ups and adolescents. The very young and the rather elderly are his audience. As a boy, he used to say that there were only two things he really wanted to do—'raise kids and dogs'. He has done both. His chow, asleep, was the model for the Dopey sequences in *Snow White*. The letters he gets from children all over the world are his special pride. He has the freedom of many cities, and the honorary degree of several universities, but the thing he values most is his enfranchisement in the ancient company of children.

Walter Elias Disney was born in Chicago in 1901; most properly, just before Christmas. His father was an Irish-Canadian, his mother of German-American stock. When Walt was two years old, his family moved to a farm in Missouri. There the boy grew up, and attended a little country school. In his free time he took to watching the animals in the fields and barnyard, trying to catch their movements on paper. He always loved to draw, but in an impatient, perfunctory way, with long, fluent lines. He would snatch a piece of paper and a stub of pencil, as he does now, and rough out an animated sketch. He likes to do everything quickly, on the wing. His brother and business manager, Roy, says he has always been an impressionist.

Walt Disney was nine years old and delivering newspapers when it first occurred to him to become a cartoonist. He was seventeen and working as a postman when he grew convinced of it. He had already taken some night-school lessons in cartoon-drawing with Leroy Gossitt, an artist on the old *Chicago Tribune* staff. Too young to enlist in the first World War, he went to France as a Red Cross ambulance driver. His ambulance was quickly covered with emphatic Disney sketches.

Home again, in Kansas, Walt joined an advertising agency which did work for farm journals. He specialised in drawing egg-laying mash, salt blocks for cattle, and farm equipment. Aspiring to higher things, he took a job with a firm that turned out advertising slides and films for motion picture theatres. His boss let him take home an old camera that was lying about in the office. Walt and a friend rigged up a studio in an unused garage and started experimenting. Their idea was to make short animated cartoons of well-known fairy-tales. *Little Red Riding-Hood* was their first choice.

Mickey Mouse was conceived in that garage studio in Kansas City, and born in another garage studio in Hollywood. After various tentative experiments in the cartoon field, with *Alice*, *Oswald the Lucky Rabbit*, and other fairy-tale subjects, Walt decided to set up his own company in Hollywood, with the help of his brother Roy. They took over another old garage, stands and tables were run up out of packing cases, Roy was taught to use the camera, and Walt and his friends spent their days drawing furiously.

Looking about for a new character, Walt remembered a mouse that used to come out for crumbs on his desk in Kansas City. It had always seemed to him a mouse with a personality. He had called it Mortimer. But now, as he began to draw the little creature and got to know him intimately, the name seemed too formal. He changed it to Mickey. Two silent films were made with Mickey Mouse, and attracted no attention, because the year was 1928 and talkies were sweeping the country. In the third cartoon, *Steamboat Willie*, Disney introduced sound, and the mouse and the man together took the world by storm.

One must put the mouse before the man, because the story of the Disney cartoons is a success story in which the artist has been increasingly dwarfed by his creatures. Today, Walt Disney is an incorporated company, associated with toys, books, hardware, and even gas-masks, with studios sprawling over many acres and employing many hundreds of hands. Its animal stars—a mouse, a duck, and a dog, a cricket, a deer, and an elephant—are household familiars all over the globe; its films are regularly translated into eighteen languages.

Disney cartoons provide material for newspaper serials, government propaganda campaigns, toothmugs, and television broadcasts; they have been quoted in sermons and editorials, and are considered fair game for the very best critics. If Disney makes a hit today it is no longer news; but if he makes a mistake it is a tragic blunder. This is success.

As the organisation has grown larger and larger, Walt himself, in the public eye, has become more and more of a diminished figure. This pale, slight, elusive, curiously tongue-tied American has no sort of genius for personal publicity. He lets other people talk for him, which has given the impression that he has nothing to say. He lets other people draw for him, which has led to the legend that he cannot draw. His own fancies are so clear in his own mind that he treats them with a flippant affection which often makes him appear to be slightly mad. It is absurd for Disney to say that he is going to Ireland to find a leprechaun, but right that he should feel he is. It is preposterous for the head of Disney Inc. to go on playing the voice of Mickey Mouse, but splendid that he should want to do such a thing.

The secret of Walt Disney is that he has a talent for smallness, not for greatness. His mind is only very lightly cultivated. He is uneasy in the presence of mature thought and large art. He is like a child who has a passion for tiny toys, finding them all the more lovable because they are at once so perfect and so small. He charms old people because he recalls the magic of their early days. He delights children, because it is natural in him to see life child-size, with all the best gifts in the world bunched tight into a Christmas stocking.

POST-WAR EUROPE

JEAN-PAUL SARTRE

JEAN-PAUL SARTRE is now the most read and most discussed of living French authors. In Paris the works of Gide, Paulhan, and Michaux are to be had anywhere: Sartre is sold out. Even in the reading-room of the Bibliothèque Nationale, all books by him are usually unobtainable. His plays are widely translated and produced in many countries. Sartre's recent career (he is over forty) has been a lightning flash. Is there real fuel and abiding power as well?

The son of a naval officer, who died when he was very young, Sartre lives with his mother in a flat in the rue Bonaparte, a noisy, cheerful little street. He went to school and university in Paris; and in 1929, having graduated, he became a schoolmaster at Le Havre and at Laon, and finally at the Condorcet, Paris. Having never taken a doctorate, he is not eligible for a university Chair. Probably the Sorbonne would never have him, and he, with fame and fortune all around, probably has no inclination for the Sorbonne. His own chair (with a small 'c') is much cosier.

He was called up when war broke out, and was captured in 1940 near Strasbourg: after spending a year in a prison camp in Germany, he managed to persuade the authorities there, thanks to a slight divergence in his eyes and also to an astute cooking of his Army paybook, that he was no longer fit or eligible for military service. He returned to Paris and produced a clandestine leaflet called *Socialisme et Liberté*: but it was not a great success. So he carried on with his own work, two new plays, *Les Mouches* and *Huis Clos*, being produced in Paris during the occupation.

He is a philosopher remarkable for the force, one might almost say the animal vigour, of his thought: a novelist of great fecundity and a sumptuous flow of words, mixed a little too carefully with vulgar expressions and low-class slang: a playwright able to sustain themes apparently void of dramatic interest: and a political journalist with a word to say on all contemporary problems. He now scores in every field he enters.

His Existentialism has been much debunked, light-heartedly or savagely; but specialists say he is a very sound philosopher indeed, and the last word should be with them. One would have expected, then, to find him disconcerted by the fearsome following he had at one moment, but he appeared to take great pleasure in it. He still listens to his disciples describing the meetings they have held, and the enthusiasm of audiences in the Americas or different parts of Europe, with all the glee of an Oxford Grouper who has had a full house in Tunbridge Wells or netted a stray Brigadier. He has been fanatically defended and fanatically attacked by people who had little idea of what his philosophy meant. On the one hand, there was the crowd of *étourdis*, students, polytechnic intellectuals, ladies living alone in the country, and the tousle-headed lovelies that attach themselves instinctively to high-toned periodicals in all countries: on the other, those who look upon all systematic philosophy as just another way to keep a man quiet and happy, and out of the kitchen, while someone gets on with making lunch: and who regard incapacity to seize ideas as proof of robust mental health.

But even now that the sun has gone down on the once teeming school of pseudo-existentialists, Sartre remains fashionable. This popular vogue has sprung up since the Liberation. Frenchmen, today, particularly Parisians, seem to recognise his mental climate as that of their lives. Before the war, the disgust which is the peculiar emanation of his books, the pessimism and the rootless existences of his characters, might still have seemed overdone. Today, Paris with the smell of decay over it, paralysed, frustrated, nauseated, has become in a curious way the Paris of Sartre: a capital whose tomorrow, if there is one, is still hidden in the clouds. Pessimism here is the café pessimism of Sartre, not the heroic pessimism of Malraux: and Sartre combines with it what is also greatly appreciated at the moment, an attitude of high moral indignation towards the shortcomings of others, especially politicians. As a novelist he revels in squalor, as a political journalist in wrathful indignation. This is true to the new France, where the very concierge pauses between two illicit deals to observe darkly that the people will not tolerate the existing corruption for much longer.

Sartre himself is probably one of the happiest and most 'realised' people in the country. A genuine pessimist does not pour out a stream of plays and books, but sits with his head in his hands or reaches for the bottle. His friends assert that, far from being the broody, somewhat Teutonic nihilist that one might be tempted to imagine, Sartre is always cheerful, gay, and enchanted with everything. This may largely result from the change-over from school-mastering to the life of a highly successful writer, fêted, photographed, surrounded by the admiring young, and with eager foreign journalists gathering about him wherever he settles like wasps on a ripe plum. Once he crept out to a café in search of a little warmth and a place to write; now there is the study in the rue Bonaparte.

He used to be a familiar figure in the Café Flore, a squalid little place with low ceilings and ignoble furniture, much frequented by literary ladies and young men with their hair dressed in the long rolling bob of which Parisian coiffeurs have the secret, and, as often as not, with ancient copies of the *Daily Worker* thrust into their pockets; and by German Jews, either humble and reverent or themselves frowning portentously over piles of grubby manuscript; and American women smoking pipes, and tramps trying to borrow an odd coin. Nowadays he prefers the Bar Pont Royale, close to the office where he edits *Les Temps Modernes.* Here all is comfort and brown leather, arty ashtrays, diffused lighting, with a vast bowl of artificial flowers at one end and a hideous strip of stained glass at the other, where the radio drools eternally on in an atmosphere of a comfortable roadhouse, and drinks start around Fr. 90. Will this change of atmosphere mean change of thought and a new Sartre-style literature, exuberantly petit-bourgeois?

What is certain is that Sartre as a proletarian, as a revolutionary, does not come off. His doctrine of 'engagement' finds no response among those who are engaged willy-nilly, and they do not read him any more than the other literary intellectuals with elaborate ideas for their welfare: their own organs regularly launch the bitterest of attacks upon him. The class in which he is truly at home, even while savouring the horror of it to the last drop, is his own.

KURT SCHUMACHER

IN the almost-forgotten days of 1931—when Weimar Germany was dominated by the rival campaigns of Nazis and Communists—three young Social Democrat members of the Reichstag dedicated themselves to reviving the German Labour movement. Their names were Mierendorff, Haubach, and Schumacher.

Unlike the older leaders of the Social Democrat Party, they were keenly aware of the impending doom with which totalitarianism threatened them from two sides. They determined to shake the traditional German labour movement from its petty preoccupation with wages and its narrow neo-Marxist outlook. They wanted to inspire it with a will to live and a will to fight.

They named their revivalist effort the Iron Front and took as their symbol three upward-pointing arrows. They failed completely to check the rising tide of Nazism. But the virility of their effort led to the adoption of their symbol by other European Socialist Parties—it was to be seen in the buttonholes of French, Polish, and Austrian socialists after 1945.

When Hitler came to power in 1933 none of these three men surrendered; and none of them went abroad. Within a few months they were prisoners in concentration camps. The treatment which the S.S. gave to their political opponents is now well known (though at the time a morally lazy world hardly bothered to read the reports which were published outside Germany).

They were humiliated and ill-used with sadistic inhumanity during the long years that Hitler was impressing everyone by his motor-roads and mass ceremonies. After six years, two of them—Mierendorff and Haubach—were let out, just before the war. With the greatest courage they made contact with the secret resistance movement, which was to culminate unsuccessfully in the 20 July plot. Mierendorff was killed in an air-raid before the plot matured; Haubach was hanged after it failed in January, 1945.

The third, Kurt Schumacher, was not let out of concentration camp until the spring of 1943. A one-armed man (he lost an arm in the first World War) coming from concentration camp at that date was too conspicuous a colleague for the plotters to accept, as it was obvious that he was closely watched. Nevertheless, the Gestapo re-arrested him in August 1944 in their reprisal 'Operation Thunderstorm'. But he was not one of the thousands—the number is estimated at between three and four thousand—of Germans executed in the last months of the Nazi régime.

Schumacher's endurance of ten years of concentration camp without yielding, gradually made him a legendary figure in the fragmented resistance groups which existed throughout the Nazi régime. How he had refused to sign a promise not to meet his former comrades if released; how he was nearly made blind in Dachau; how, with a frail body and at the mercy of the camp guards he went on a hunger strike for twenty-nine days rather than do forced labour and won, these stories were passed from the soulless camps hidden in pine forests to working-class tenements in Berlin and Hamburg.

Today, in his early fifties, Kurt Schumacher is the elected spokesman of the whole Social Democrat Party of Germany; he lives an ascetic life at bombed Hanover, in three rooms, and with no car. He has largely contributed to three important political developments. First, a large Social Democrat Party (S.P.D.) has been re-created, numbering 600,000 members in the Western Zone—despite lack of the means to move and communicate freely, the public apathy of a collapsed society, and many obstructions by the Allies in the early months. Secondly, 'fusion' with the Communists has been resisted on grounds of democratic principle and humanist behaviour—despite the intimidating effect of compulsory 'fusion' in the Russion Zone. Thirdly, the Social Democrat Party has been committed to a much bolder socialist policy than the old 'more wages' programme, which failed between the wars.

Schumacher has long made up his mind that the central theme of his domestic policy should be 'equality of sacrifice' or a fair distribution of the burden of defeat. For this reason the S.P.D. is pressing for a progressive capital levy. This has been the subject of one of the strongest S.P.D. complaints against British occupation policy.

In the relations of Germany to the victors, Dr Schumacher from the first hour attacked the 'Morgenthau policy' of reducing Germany to poverty and demanded the chance to build up an economy capable of providing a decent standard of living. His party's mission, Schumacher argued, was to prevent a rebirth of German nationalism; that could not be achieved by inflicting grievances and miseries on succeeding generations.

The man who has become so prominent in contemporary Germany looks, at first sight, a physical wreck. As thin as a skeleton, with uneven eyes burning in a sunken face, he seems to symbolise the double suffering of those who were Hitler's victims and now must share in paying for Hitler's deeds. But his prodigious energy drives him on. On the public platform his passionate sincerity and self-dedication transform the impression he makes from that of a martyr to that of a prophet.

He is a highly effective speaker, ironical, caustic, epigrammatic, and most telling in attack. Whether his target is the Communists, the rightist Christian-Democrats, or British Military Government itself, he does not mince his words. Probably 'Mil. Gov.' sitting in the seats of power finds it easier to forgive his biting criticism than do his German political opponents. Whether Schumacher can move on from political campaigning, in which his heroism should never be forgotten, to the very different tasks of Government, in which coalition is sometimes and compromise is always necessary, time and the Allies may some day give him a chance to show.

MOMENTS MUSICAUX

TOSCANINI

SIGNOR TOSCANINI is the last person who would ever have dreamt of becoming what today he undoubtedly is: a legend, and a political symbol. For all his life belongs to music, and there is hardly an artist who has so effaced his self in the service of his art as Toscanini has in the service of music.

Music is not only his profession. It is his religion, his hobby, and also his vice. (He is as free from the ordinary modern mass-hobbies and vices as any dictator. To an American reporter who once inquired into the reasons for his not smoking he answered gallantly: 'I smoked my first cigarette and kissed my first woman on the same day. I have never had time for tobacco since'.)

Even unschooled listeners perceive, almost without fail, that every piece of music conducted by Toscanini sounds different: more penetrating, more translucent, more fully real; as if a landscape which one has only known under a clouded sky is suddenly pierced to its last folds by an exuberant sun. (One criticism sometimes made of Toscanini is that some musical landscapes are meant to be cloud-covered.)

Musical connoisseurs usually record a further experience: that every reading of Toscanini's has a curiously compelling air of authenticity about it. You never feel—as with almost every other great conductor—the presence of a third personality and temperament between yourself and the composer: you feel confronted with the very essence of the work—with the truth and nothing but the truth; with musical anatomy laid faithfully bare, as in a nude study of Leonardo's, with every tiniest muscle playing in the golden light. Is it illusion? Then it is a curiously cogent illusion.

What is Toscanini's secret? Part of it is a sober and practical, prosaic matter: rehearsal time. Toscanini based his career as a conductor on the conviction that it must be possible to regain in the large orchestras of modern times the purity and precision of execution which prevailed in the small virtuoso court ensembles of the eighteenth century. But it would require harder work, many more rehearsals, and more critical scrutiny of the individual player. Toscanini has always insisted with an unshakable determination on practically unlimited rehearsal time. After thirty rehearsals of Beethoven's Mass in D with the orchestra and choir of La Scala, he eventually put away his baton and said quietly: 'Ladies and gentlemen—next year.' And that was in 1927, the centenary of Beethoven's death, when all Italy had waited for this performance!

What makes orchestras 'take' his impatient insistence on perfection is his complete lack of vanity. He never seeks the 'effect' which shows off the conductor; he never makes a gesture for the benefit of the audience's back-view of him; he never bows alone. Once an orchestra applauded him during rehearsal after he had made them play a difficult passage in a way they themselves had never known; he looked up distressed and bewildered: 'But for God's sake, that's not me; that's Beethoven.'

His complete and medium-like absorption in the works he conducts is helped by his memory, and this in turn he partly owes to a defect. In his youth he was handicapped by extreme shortsightedness; he could not rely on reading music; he had to learn it by heart—first his parts as a 'cellist, then his scores as a conductor. He thus developed his formidable and by now legendary musical memory. He never appears with a score at a performance; he carries his musical library in his head. But this he has only been able to keep up by identifying himself with the works in an uncanny manner—by re-living, re-feeling, almost re-creating them on behalf of their composers.

Conducting the Bayreuth orchestra, he once stopped at a certain point in *Tristan*: 'This *appoggiatura* does not exist.' 'It's written here,' said the players and brought him the score. Toscanini nosed it. 'That's a printing error', he insisted. The high priests of the Wagnerian cult were indignant. For years and years they had played that *appoggiatura*. Toscanini ordered

Wagner's manuscript to be taken out of the library. There it was, the little note; but cancelled with a hardly perceptible stroke in faded ink by the composer's hand.

Perhaps this almost uncanny absorption in, and self-identification with, the works of others explains why Toscanini, unlike so many other great conductors, has never been tempted to write music of his own.

Some critics feel that Toscanini's *tempi* are too quick; and he himself admits it sometimes. 'Provided that air can circulate between the notes', he says.

He once had a bet with the Italian conductor Bernardino Molinari about the ideal duration of Ravel's *Bolero*. Molinari said it should last sixteen minutes, Toscanini fifteen. They wired to Ravel who cabled back: 'sixteen'. Toscanini paid, but could not refrain from sending another telegram to Ravel: 'You are wrong'. A more valid criticism of Toscanini is perhaps that his executions are too rigidly serious. Sometimes, even classic composers indulge in self-parody and wit; and sometimes they might even have liked a little fun or nonsense. But Toscanini always plays them with unvarying earnest and grim fidelity and precision.

Of course, his background is 'left' in any case. His father, a tailor in 'red' Parma, had fought under Garibaldi, and was a diehard Radical. But young Toscanini nearly forgot politics for music. It was only when politics—totalitarian politics—intruded upon music that the ageing maestro found himself, reluctantly, forced into resistance and final revolt—which has now made him a symbol of militant anti-Fascism the world over.

For years under Mussolini's hated régime Toscanini stayed at La Scala: fighting Fascist interference at every step, but still putting up with some of it for the sake of his music. He did, after all, conduct *Giovinezza* for years at the opening of opera nights. It was only when the Fascists tried to force him to play their hymn at a memorial concert, where the gesture would, on top of its political insincerity, have been a gross lapse of musical taste, that he refused. And then followed that ghastly incident when the local Fascist leader publicly hit him in the face, then the withdrawal of his passport, finally his break with his country. From then onward he became the great exile, the great living protest against the artistic barbarity—and thus, finally, against the general barbarity—of the new tyrannies.

When Hitler came to power, and Jewish music and musicians were banned in Germany, Toscanini's signature was the first under a solemn indictment of this outrage. He no longer went to Bayreuth. He wrote to the Director of the Wagner Memorial: 'I burn, I freeze, but I cannot be lukewarm.' When the Nazis seized Austria, he also withdrew from the Salzburg festivals. Instead, he went, unpaid, to Tel-Aviv to help Bronislaw Huberman organise a Jewish orchestra.

In the night of 25 July 1943, when Mussolini fell, the crowds in the streets of Milan shouted 'Viva Toscanini', as they had one century earlier shouted 'Viva Verdi' in the face of the Austrian gendarmes: a great musician had once more become the impersonation of the fight for freedom.

Toscanini became a politician *malgré lui*, in the defence of music; and his greatest and purest triumph is that today he is once more leading the re-created Scala to the artistic heights on which it had dwelt in happier times.

RICHARD STRAUSS

It is now more than fifty years ago that Richard Strauss made his first appearance in London. Then he was about the wildest of the wild young men of Continental music—one of those outsiders on whom London, with its mixture of curiosity, broad-mindedness, and business shrewdness, so often places a little side-bet while the odds are long. When he came next, seven years later, to conduct a festival of his own music, he was the scream and the rage of musical fashion of the day. Another seven years, and the composer of *Rosenkavalier* had become the darling of the wealthy music-loving public, while the young high-brows and musical revolutionaries were just beginning to sniff at him. All this was well before 1914.

Strauss was a revolutionary in youth, who turned Conservative in middle age. But throughout both periods he remained essentially the same man: very middle class, very much the master-craftsman, clear-minded, conscientious, not hypocritically disdainful of worldly and material success, but quite without 'artistic' vanity, and impatient of anything he regarded as swindle and pretension. His father, horn-player in the Munich orchestra, was reputedly one of the best horn-players of his time. The son transferred the same ethos and ambition of craftsmanship to a wider musical field.

Perhaps his conducting is the best key to his personality. Strauss may be a 'showy' composer—being of the middle class, not the aristocracy, he happens to believe in pomp and circumstance—but he is the least showy conductor imaginable. Knowing that a conductor's work is done at rehearsal-time, he almost extinguishes himself at the desk during the concert. No posturing to impress the uninstructed public; and yet his interpretations, especially of Mozart, touch perfection.

His attitude to his work as a composer is similar: no fuss about genius and inspiration; just the quiet, slightly cynical self-confidence of the accomplished master-craftsman. Mahler, when presented with the score of *Salome*, found to his astonishment that the climax, the dance, was missing. 'Oh yes', said Strauss. 'It did not come off yet. But I'll fix that all right.' He has at all times of his life worked prodigiously, but somehow phlegmatically; without fury and ecstasy in times of inspiration, without despair in drier times; always keeping a sober eye on the commercial returns of his work, but never stooping to the malodorous business machinations of, say, Beethoven.

He had the wisdom never to indulge in musical polemics—the fiercest and most inconclusive of all polemics—and never to mix in politics. This saved him from the sad lot of Mengelberg in being cut off from musical activity for non-musical reasons, and the sadder lot of Toscanini and Casals in being tainted with the praise of dubious propagandists for dubious motives. He accepted the position of Hofkapellmeister under the Kaiser, but when the Kaiser held forth on modern music, answered quietly: 'Your Majesty will not expect me to share your opinions.' Just so he was President of the Reich Chamber of Music under Hitler, but quietly asked the Jewish émigré Stefan Zweig to write him a libretto for a new opera. When Zweig replied that this opera would stand little chance of performance in the Third Reich, he answered confidently (a wrong political forecast): 'Till our opera is finished, the Third Reich will be forgotten.' His letter was intercepted, but no action taken. The great man was too old and too famous for Goebbels to wish to martyrise him gratuitously.

Some of his music—*Salome, Elektra*—reaches extremes in the musical expression of morbid hysteria and homicidal or suicidal passion. But there is a certain objectivity in this expression, and at the time he composed *Salome* Strauss took a bet with Mahler that he could equally well express in music the exact sensation of putting down a glass of foaming iced Munich beer. (Later, in his opera *Intermezzo*, he came very near to doing it.) The cool, faintly humorous, faintly cynical look of his slightly protruding eyes always seemed somewhat to belie the more outrageously passionate passages of his music; and the composer of *Don Juan*, and *A Hero's Life* was all the time unashamedly a good family man, cheerfully and almost demonstratively philistine in his private habits, cynically witty at the expense of any bohemian ostentation, keeping regular hours, unbending to simple pleasures, and proud of his mastery in the game of Skat, the German equivalent of Whist.

Such a nature admirably fitted him for standing the long siege of public disfavour during his maturity. To this day the later work of this world-famous composer is almost unknown. The enormous popularity of *Rosenkavalier* has prevented most people from discovering its, in many respects, superior later companion-piece, *Arabella*. And how many of those who sniff at *The Woman Without a Shadow*, *The Egyptian Helena*, *The Silent Woman*, or *The Day of Peace* as mere routine-output of the Strauss factory could quote one single melody from them?

It is true that these later works have brought no startling new developments in Strauss's style, still less any compromises with the nervously changing fashions of their period. It is true that, in their sumptuousness, erudition, glossiness, rich slickness, and sensuous refinement, they are pre-1914 rather than pre-1939. But today, when the 'twenties and 'thirties are beginning to be as much 'period' as the 'teens, this ceases to matter very much. And to the musical public of, say, 2000, it will be as irrelevant as it is to us that Bach, in the seventeen forties, was widely considered hopelessly out of date and behind his times, and referred to as 'the old perruque' by his more progressive and fashionable sons.

To compare Richard Strauss with Bach of all masters may, under many aspects, look preposterous. But there are some likenesses: the honest craftsman's approach to their art, the objectivity and conscientiousness of their mastery, the fidelity to their own style and their own times, the unflagging productivity into old age. These are grand qualities; and in paying tribute to them, musical London, in its Strauss season of autumn 1947, gave proof of discernment and maturity.

HINDEMITH

AFTER seven years of fruitful exile in America, where he has been composing, playing, teaching, and theorising as copiously as a dozen eighteenth-century *Kapellmeisters* rolled into one, Paul Hindemith has revisited the Europe whose shores he left with the proud imprimatur of Nazi ridicule.

Was Hindemith in those days aesthetically of the extreme Left? Goebbels had no hesitation in labelling him as such. The composer of the Philharmonic Concerto and *Mathis der Maler* was awarded first place among Germany's 'cultural Bolsheviks' and 'musical nihilists'. Vilification was turned on at full cock.

No campaign could have been more fatuous. We see that very plainly now on reading such unexceptionable works as *Traditional Harmony* and *Elementary Training for Musicians*, which were written between composition classes at Yale University; but even ten years ago it was as plain as a pikestaff to anybody with a milligram of common sense that Hindemith's polyphony had much more in common with Europe's central musical tradition than the mock-Wagnerian trash which then enjoyed Party patronage.

His last works are at times almost bluff and back-slapping in their approach. Their idiom, one suspects, would have been alien, perhaps repugnant, to the ruthless Hindemith of the 'twenties. In those days his wit and erudition had a harsher edge.

It was in the early 'thirties that a semi-romantic note began to echo through Hindemith's scores. His harmony and his melodic line developed a certain Gothic quality, redolent of gargoyles and Nuremberg half-timbering. Foes and friends were not wanting who said, 'Aha! Hindemith is tempering his art to Nazi ideology. He's going neo-romantic, folky and nationalistic at Hitler's bidding.' This slander was no less silly than the parallel Nazi accusation of cultural anarchism. All who were close to Hindemith in those years of flux and strain bear witness to his utter artistic and personal integrity.

At no stage in his career has Hindemith's art been a simple thing to diagnose. It is a complex of classical streaks, romantic survivals, and traditional loyalties, with strong innovatory trends superadded. The most cursory glance at his career suffices to show the multitudinousness of the man. Of general education in the formal sense he had little. He picked up Latin, Greek, English, French in oddments of spare time. Music lessons were subsidised by playing in cinemas and theatres. By 1915, when he became leader of the Frankfort Opera orchestra at the age of twenty, he could play practically every musical instrument known to man. The viola became his favourite. As a member of the Amar-Hindemith string quartet he widely toured Central Europe from the early 1920s onward.

Music of all kinds poured from his pen. One of the kinds was labelled *Gebrauchsmusik*—utility music. Composers, argued the young Hindemith, must come down from their ivory towers and mix with the crowd. Instead of locking themselves aloofly away and spreading their delicately-nurtured souls on perfumed manuscript paper, they must be ready to make themselves useful in humble, even humdrum, channels. Thus we find Hindemith cheerfully putting his name between 1920 and 1930 to music written for mechanical organ, children's games, pianola, community singing, Felix the Cat films, and a clown show. Topicality did not scare him—he wrote music to celebrate the Lindbergh flight; nor did modern dance idioms—a 1922 piano suite, for example, includes a 'shimmy' movement.

One does not wish to exaggerate the importance of Hindemith's *Gebrauchsmusik* phase. It was exaggerated more than enough at the time. Simultaneously he was creating a succession of sober and solid works whose technical resource (whatever their aesthetic worth—a matter of continuing debate) merits comparison with that of J. S. Bach himself. This Bach comparison comes inevitably to the lips of all who give patient hearing to Hindemith's major works. The affinity is especially evident in the monumental *Ludus Tonalis*, a sequence of twelve fugues with prologue, epilogue and interludes, scored for solo piano, muscular hands, stout heart and first-class brain.

A heaven-sent teacher, Hindemith taught Composition at the

Hochschule für Musik, Berlin. Each student had to emulate his master by playing, with some degree of proficiency, every instrument in the orchestra. He was expected into the bargain to compose now and again a two-minute piece for scratch student bands of varying composition. One week the band would be a refined array of strings and flutes. Next week it would be a raucous compound of trumpets, trombones, saxophones and the like. In trying out the efforts of fledgling composers, these Robber Bands, as Hindemith called them, made shocking noises but provided all parties with valuable lessons, mostly of a negative sort.

When the Nazis came to power, Hindemith made no attempt to hide his disdain for the parvenus. Nor did he cease to associate with Jewish artists or to cultivate young Jewish talent. It was his way on entering the *Hochschule* in the morning either to refrain from the obligatory heiling and saluting or to put on an alternative performance which always fetched a conniving grin from the hall-porter. He would shout 'Hitler!' with a grimace, at the same time making a downward slapping motion with his right hand, as though chastising a tiresome dog.

The storm duly broke in the kept press of 1934. Furtwängler, the conductor, courageously defended Hindemith, first in print, then in the teeth of the Führer himself at Bayreuth during the 1936 Wagner festival. It seems that Furtwängler told Hitler that men of genius are too few in this world to be banned. The anti-Hindemith campaign was presumptuous. The whole of German youth, the *Hitlerjugend* included, stood solidly behind Hindemith, their idol.

Hitler flew into one of his apocalyptic rages, naturally. A film of insanity was spreading and thickening over the Third Reich. Nothing that Furtwängler could do would pierce it. Hindemith went on thinking and writing music, an enclave of calm in the centre of uproar. Quietly he made his preparations to withdraw from a country which demanded of its men of genius that they should become bakelite megaphones.

The composition class at Yale is the *Hochschule* over again with worshipful students singing and playing not only scores of their own devising but also medieval music on archaic instruments exhumed from museums. Hindemith's theoretical writings in America have brought a puzzled stare to the faces of certain of his early followers. Atonality? There's no such thing—unless you care to call sheer harmonic disorder by that name. Polytonality? But every simultaneous combination of sounds must have a harmonic root—and one root only. Polytonality is at best a rather futile sort of game. Not by any stretch of imagination can it be called a practical principle of composition. And so on.

At fifty-one Paul Hindemith is undoubtedly a mellower personality than the indefatigable compiler of utility models who set Europe by the ears thirty years ago. Critics who were scandalised then are respectful now. There has been no change of heart; no artistic *volte-face*. Whatever changes have come over Hindemith's music have been a logical unfolding. One foresees that twenty years hence the former anarch of Goebbels's malignant imagination will be loudly pedestalled as a Grand Old Man of two continents.

BENJAMIN BRITTEN

At the infantile age of thirty-two, with *Peter Grimes* trailing its clouds of gloom and glory from Sweden to Massachusetts, Benjamin Britten has behind him a career which (let this be frankly faced) makes those of most British composers appear quietly parochial by comparison.

You would not gather anything of the sort by looking at him. The world may be Britten's stage, but there is no strut, no plume, no swagger.

One shakes hands with an amiable young man whose talk is poised and polite. Nice hair; ready, easy smile; a salient and sagacious nose; clothes that are casual but not incorrect.

One sees thousands of Brittens around the Bank and Mansion House at nine any morning with bowler and umbrella, a copy of *The Times* under the oxter. The social diagnostician would place him as a junior-partner solicitor or Civil Servant halfway up the departmental rungs, with a taste for etchings, progressive politics, and week-end tennis.

The only hint of unusualness is about the heavy-lidded eyes. Britten gives the impression of a man who habitually averts his regard from the distracting shows of the outer world that he may concentrate upon inner pageantries. This is no flight of fancy. Britten's primary workshop is his head, which remains as unflurried and as active as a gyroscope amid the comings and goings of an agitated physical existence.

When not flying or sailing to foreign opera houses and concert halls Britten is perpetually rushing off to catch trains for voice-and-piano recitals with Peter Pears in remote provincial towns. The business of musical creation goes on serenely among the bustle and the baggage. Looking unseeingly through train windows at speeding landscapes and symbolical staves of telegraph wires, Britten composes as fluently as if he were sitting in a soundproof cell, with quires of manuscript paper before him and a grand piano at his elbow.

'First', he says, 'I sit down and conceive the idea of a piece. By "idea" I mean the structural plan—form, moods, contrasts, textures, key systems. Then I work out the details; embody the idea in notes. Usually I have the music complete in my head before putting pen to paper.'

Between bouts of concert-giving and preparation, Britten retires to Snape, near Aldeburgh, in his native Suffolk. Two years before the war he bought an ancient windmill at Snape. What was left of the sails and the rotating wooden box he dismantled. The circular brick base he turned into a study. The walls are lined with books. There is a piano. This is Britten's ivory tower, made of mellow brick, one story high.

Here he stays for a month or two at a stretch, setting down on paper the music he has been secreting and perfecting in his mind's ear. If the medium is simple, such as string quartet or unaccompanied four-part chorus, he writes it down straight away in full score, much as if he were writing a letter. In the case of a more complex medium—an operatic scena, for example, with soloists, chorus and orchestra—he writes a complete short-score version. Everything is there, in a kind of musical shorthand intelligible only to Britten himself, from piccolo on the top line to string basses at the bottom. Short-score is transcribed and expanded at leisure into full-score, a laborious, clerkly business.

That Britten does not build up from sketches is significant. Sketch-book technique sometimes leads to fragmentary brilliance. A typical Britten movement, on the other hand, has a bigness and coherence of build which may be readily traced to his technique of meditation. In first shaping the whole, then working down through the parts to the details, he employs a procedure that makes for logic and simplicity of structure.

Britten's success has been resounding. Like all resounding successes, it does not go unchallenged. Some consider that his very copiousness excludes a uniformly high quality. At the age of twelve, when he was sent to Gresham's School, he had written ten piano sonatas, six string quartets, an oratorio, and dozens of songs. His mother wanted him to study music, but his father, a Lowestoft dental surgeon, was in favour of his taking up mathematics. His early musical talent came to the notice of the late Frank Bridge about this time, and during school holidays Bridge gave the young Britten lessons. While still a boy Britten entered the Royal College of Music, London, working with John Ireland for composition and Arthur Benjamin for piano. His first commissions were for music for broadcast plays and films. The fountain has been playing at full pressure, the basin running over, ever since.

It is not to be denied that mawkish or pedestrian pages occasionally occur. The brittle music of Tarquin's ride in *The Rape* compares oddly with the exquisite vocal patternings for Lucretia and her serving women which follow. And who will pretend that the melodramatic murmurings of Mrs Sedley ('Murder most foul it is . . .') in the last act of *Peter Grimes* are on the same level—in the same world, even—as Grimes's monologue, 'Now the Great Bear and the Pleiades', and the brooding canon which accompanies it on the strings?

The latter is one of the great pages of contemporary music. Like most of Britten's music it is curiously impersonal. Here we have music without fingerprints. Britten may, indeed, be regarded as representing the English wing of the movement away from egocentricity and back to traditional formulas which began a quarter of a century ago with Stravinsky's *Pulcinella*. He is not in the least concerned to write music that expresses his personality. His sole concern is to write music which shall be apt and engrossing in its own terms.

To this end he makes himself free of the entire musical armoury. The idiom of *Grimes* ranges from *The Rite of Spring* to Schubert. For *This Way to the Tomb!* he wrote austere ecclesiastical polyphony and a hot swing interlude for piano and percussion outfit which would have done credit to Duke Ellington. In the choral setting of Auden's *Hymn to St Cecilia* there is an accompanied soprano-solo ('O dear white children. . . .') of aerial beauty which, technically considered, might have been written by Sterndale Bennett or Arthur Sullivan. To court such affinities in 1942 argued a revolutionary boldness.

Britten is frank about his eclecticism. When the matter was mentioned to him by the present writer, he replied:

'It is largely a matter of when one was born. If I had been

born in 1813 instead of 1913 I should have been a romantic, primarily concerned to express my personality in music. . . .

'The rot (if that isn't too strong a word) began with Beethoven. Before Beethoven, music served things greater than itself—the glory of God or the glory of the State, for example. After Beethoven, the composer was the centre of his own universe. The romantics became so intensely personal that it looked as though we were going to reach a point at which the composer would be the only man capable of understanding his own music!

'Then came Picasso and Stravinsky. They loosened up painting and music, freed them from the tyranny of the purely personal. They passed from manner to manner as a bee passes from flower to flower.'

'And you', it was suggested 'do much the same thing?'

'I do not see why I should lock myself inside a purely personal idiom,' said Britten. 'I write in the manner best suited to the words, theme, or dramatic situation which I happen to be handling.'

Such notions would have been plumb heretical in Bloomsbury between the wars. Even now there are many who consider them wrongheaded. This should reassure Mr Britten. There is no composer of enduring merit who has not been regarded as wrongheaded in his day.